"This collection is as exhilarating and heartbreaking and unforgettable as first love, itself. I have a major crush on *Crush*—what a complex dreamboat of a book."

—Gayle Brandeis, author of *My Life with the Lincolns* and *Delta Girls*

"With humor, with courage, with sweet tender hearts, these twenty-six writers remind us of the infinite numbers of ways love can make us feel so alive yet so vulnerable."

—Diana Joseph, author of *I'm Sorry You Feel That Way*

"What's more captivating than a crush? An anthology on the subject. No reader should resist this chance to look into the secret, stirring heart of these great writers. Romantic bedevilment has never been more accessible or abundant. Like a lover reading a long-awaited mash note, you'll feel electricity screaming through your body as you consume every impassioned word."

—Lily Burana, author of *I Love a Man in Uniform*, *Try* and *Strip City*

"There are few rapturously high moments in everyday life, and the first raw feelings of being in love, in lust, in true and honest need of another person are the highest. With *Crush*, Nicki Richesin brings us some two dozen voices captured on that cusp, and the result is an exhilaration, a wonderful collection."

—Ashley Warlick, author of *The Summer After June* and *Seek The Living*

Also available from Andrea N. Richesin and Harlequin

WHAT I WOULD TELL HER:
28 Devoted Dads on Bringing Up,
Holding On To and Letting Go of Their Daughters

BECAUSE I LOVE HER:
34 Women Writers Reflect on the Mother-Daughter Bond

Edited by
Andrea N. Richesin

# crush

26 Real-Life
Tales of
First Love

# crush

ISBN-13: 978-0-373-89233-4

Library of Congress Cataloging-in-Publication Data
Crush : 26 Real-life tales of first love/edited by Andrea N. Richesin.
    p. cm.
ISBN 978-0-373-89233-4 (pbk.)

1. Unrequited love—Anecdotes. 2. Interpersonal relations—Anecdotes. 3. Fantasy—Anecdotes. I. Richesin, Andrea N.

BF575.U57C78 2010

306.7—dc22

www.Harlequin.com

**Printed in U.S.A.**

For two of the greatest loves of my life, my grandparents,

Yvonne Burlingame
(1926–2010)

Orson Burlingame
(1920–2011)

The beauty of the world...has two edges, one of laughter, one of anguish, cutting the heart asunder.

—Virginia Woolf, *A Room of One's Own*, 1929

# contents

# crush

# introduction

I was sixteen the first time I fell in love. He was one year older with long hair the color of honey, a rakish grin and bold blue eyes. On our first date, he took me to a dinner theater to see Neil Simon's *Last of the Red Hot Lovers*. Afterward, he pushed me against my parents' front door to kiss me, scratching my cheek with his stubbled chin. He told me he had never felt this way before yet I kept asking him to prove his love to me. So he offered grand romantic gestures: poetry and carefully drawn portraits, a turquoise ring and impassioned mix tapes. To meet my conservative parents on Halloween, his costume was a T-shirt emblazoned with the symbol for anarchy. He could not have been more irresistible to me.

As suddenly as it had begun, it ended with a phone call. I was too humiliated and stunned to ask for an explanation. My mother told me to mourn him as if he were dead, which was difficult as I passed him daily in the hallways at school. Holding his hand, I had felt invincible, all the problems of the adult world far, far away. I fell in love many times afterward, but never with the same fierce feeling of abandon and certainty. I knew that love was vulnerable, a fragile aspiration I might crush if held too tightly.

Like most teenagers who've been crushed by first love, I found an imperfect path back to trust. We've all had our hearts broken and know that sinking feeling the next morning when you realize you're on your own again. You don't die of a broken heart, you only wish you could. So I suppose my mother was right, it is like a minor death—the loss of a dream, and the realization that love doesn't last forever.

Although wrestling with the demons of unrequited love is devastating, a crush can also boost a wounded ego, save a marriage, and make one feel alive. It has the power to transform a shy backward kid into a bold adult. It's not only an education for a person naive in the world, it's the joy of a fantasy you may or may not choose to pursue. Crushes can live in our heads for our own secret enjoyment, but they also encourage us to take risks we might not have imagined. Falling for the wrong person, wounded, love doomed, we still search for our soul mates even when it seems they may be impossible to find.

These twenty-six contributors offer glimpses of their first love experiences in all their joy and sadness, and how they influenced their growth as both women and men. In many cases, their crushes expanded their worlds and became the means by which they burst out of the narrow and boring cocoons of their youth and into the world at large. We recognize our own loneliness and longing to connect in their tales of heartbreak and thwarted desire.

In Jacquelyn Mitchard's incredible essay, she recounts her blissful first love, barely consummated, but which consumed her for years. She concealed the passion she felt for the young boy turned soldier in his confessional letters she kept hidden. Their secret love remained sealed away for twenty years before she confronted it again. A young Ann Hood is mistaken for an older woman when her elder brother's friend, the boy in the white VW Bug, zooms into her life. They form an unlikely friendship that lasts over thirty years. Both Mitchard and Hood take comfort in the histories of their forbidden loves, that still reminds them of the young girls they once were.

The impossible idealism of love when confronted with its messy reality makes it easy to surrender to the fantasy of a crush. It allows us to exist in a sort of imaginary world with the object of our affection. In Daria Snadowsky's "To Sir Anthony, With Love," she sees the C. S. Lewis biopic film *Shadowlands* starring Anthony Hopkins and falls head over heels for the elderly actor. She discovers that "you can project all your fairy-tale illusions on a superhuman persona and fabricate a perfect, consequence-free relationship precisely because it is unattainable. I knew my make-believe life with him would serve as an ideal distraction from my humdrum nonlife in ninth grade."

Steve Almond also recognizes how we cling to this larger fantasy of who we might be to our lover and to ourselves. He thinks, "If I could be good enough for her, I could be good enough for myself. Such is the absurd fantasy that animates all our crushes, young or old." Through her correspondence with a former crush Heather Swain learns that "we created realities about each other that worked for us at the time, which in the end is what 99 percent of crushes turn out to be." When David Levithan was ambivalent, his crush helped him to face his true feelings. Levithan's essay reveals how seeing his crush free himself helped him to do the same. He confesses, "I want to remember him as he was, even if that memory's vague, and perhaps even wrong. Who he was to me matters so much more than who he actually was." According to Levithan, "the difference between a crush and love is its viability." If a romantic union doesn't last, was it merely a crush and nothing more?

The contributors learn to deal with this inevitable rejection, and although it has made trusting again that much harder, they are wiser now. Brendan Halpin is bewildered by the refrain most teenage boys must hear, "I like you as a friend," which surely must sound like the kiss of death from the lips of a girl he's yearning to kiss. Melissa Walker and Tara Bray Smith pine for the anointed golden boy from afar. In shy journal entries, doodlings and hidden diaries they detail all their devotion they can't express to their beloved crushes. Their romantic lives take a serious toll on their self-esteem and all their insecurities would seem to melt away with his approval. Through their writings, they honed their boyfriend fantasy: a handsome prince who would whisk them away from the tedium of trudging through their bored schoolgirl lives.

Trapped in an adolescent body, many young lovers turn to music to vent their frustrations and get them through their heartaches. Brendan Halpin identified with the role of angry outsiders in youth anthems that inspired passion, rebellion and longing. In Emily Franklin's mix tape, she remembers all the songs that rang true for her many relationships. Through her starstruck daydreams of Duran Duran, Katherine Center perfected the fantasy version of herself. Like most young girls, when her days were filled with feelings of teenage inadequacy, she listened to Simon Le Bon croon just for her. As she explains, "Duran Duran...will always have my devotion for teaching me about how stories offer comfort, and the imagination can create hope."

The power of a forgotten memory, i.e., a whiff of perfume, taste of beer, such nostalgia for a first crush can send us back in time. Robert Wilder returns to his suburban neighborhood when the adorable Liz Thomas seemed to represent all his heartfelt longing and teenage dreams. In an innocent game of spin the bottle, Wilder gets to kiss the girl and become a little less nerdy and a lot bolder in his affections. His nostalgic reverie is mired in the loss of loved ones, his mother and neighbors as he remembers them as they once were when they were all still young. Catherine Newman takes us on a Patrick Süskind–induced olfactory trip down memory lane. Through sniffs of freshly laundered clothing or Anaïs Anaïs, she remembers the particular smell of desire. After the birth of her two babies, she finds that "love will fill us up and spill over and we won't be able to grasp it. We can't grasp it still."

Kitty Pryde's profound influence on Christopher Coake also has the superhuman ability to power kick him back in time. When he steps into a comic book shop and picks up an old copy of *The X-Men,* he can return to his adolescence, but also something much more complex, "the ability to reach out my hand into the images in front of me; to make the unreal real." Rebecca Walker must make a difficult decision when she discovers that her dear first love is in the hospital. In the end, she determines "there are certain moments in life that should be remembered, encased in the magic of another time and space, and left alone." Perhaps preserving our pasts is another act of kindness to ourselves to be able to draw on them when we need a treasured memory to get us through our own difficult experiences.

The self-destructive acts we commit for love can often send us on an emotional tailspin. Katie Herzog movingly recounts her terrible struggle with addiction and how it caused her to lose the great love of her life. Steve Almond pursues his lady love until she is revolted by his advances. Through such exploits, they try to prove their devotion to their crushes as much as to themselves that they're worthy of love.

A few writers punish themselves by choosing the wrong partners again and again. Kerry Cohen's tattoos are painful, visible reminders of her lost loves and her endless quest to satisfy her desire for connection. She chose to hurt herself before someone else could do so. To Cohen, "a tattoo was proof of something, a suggestion of hidden things." At first, Jon Skovron's Sally Bowles–inspired temptress challenges him to face the world, to act and work, and leave his solitary days reading in his room behind. He is drawn to her larger-than-life persona and finds a respect for this damaged creature he longs to save, if only from herself. In Melissa Febos's haunting essay, she explains how she tried to protect her boyfriend from her sexually adventurous past, but her attempts didn't keep the ghosts at bay. She learns that it's futile to hide your past from your lover if you want him to know you for who you truly are. Most astutely she observes, "We want our loves to ourselves; we want to occupy the parts of them that belong to other people, other places, things that cannot be exiled because they are already gone. We harbor this desire out of selfishness, but ultimately, perhaps out of fear."

Sheila Kohler falls for the eternal bad boy, her Mr. Rochester, as she puts it. Hers is a more mature love, not the fantasy she dreamed of, but one of betrayal, love spurned and infidelity. Our hearts break for Kohler as she endures her husband's longtime dalliances. Finally, after years of neglect, she forges a meaningful partnership with her new husband. Laurie Faria Stolarz wonders what might have been in her essay. Her breakup also means the end of possibilities—of another life. In Rebecca Woolf's "Before It Gets Complicated," she questions the risk of seeking companionship outside her marriage when she randomly meets her childhood best friend at a bar twenty-six years later. She writes, "The fairy tale has taught us that true love means never having to lust after anyone else." Woolf realizes she's not willing to risk what she has, that some risks are too great.

6

In Coake's searing essay, he teaches his students about the meaning of first love and how our perspective can change with age and experience. He believes they may already have learned that "some loves we can measure only through the magnitude of their loss."

The truth is we all have our hearts broken, but we learn to try again, to keep reaching for new love wherever we can find it. In each of these tender essays, the talented contributors recognize that risking themselves makes life worth living, that the pain they feel from a broken heart keeps it beating. It beats, even when the world seems to have stopped. It beats on and on and then one day it quickens again.

Andrea N. Richesin
San Rafael, California
July 2010

# What I Kept

## Jacquelyn Mitchard

He was too old for me.

Everyone was too old for me.

Kids stayed younger longer then, but especially me.

My parents were stern. When he was a young man, my father had trained horses; and sometimes I felt I was being taught my ground manners on a long line—a sharp thwack of the whip next to my ear if I broke form. No one ever punished me. No one needed to. I knew what was expected.

I was good in school. I was pretty although not, by far, the prettiest. No one in my family, on either side, had ever graduated high school, and college was expected for me. Nothing would interfere. From wayward genes of all kinds, my parents expected to throw a Thoroughbred.

So I simply watched the tanned, beautiful boy with the hyacinth eyes as he mowed the lawn around all the hills at his grandparents' fishing resort in Michigan. His grandparents were close friends with my grandparents: they'd spent many years together—on porches thrust out over a lake, in the achromatic twilights when the water and sky formed a soft sheet with no seam. Animated by the thwack of moths that threw themselves against the lanterns and tiki lights, they drank Miller High Life and played poker while half hoping fish would tweak a lazy leaning line. All along the lake were other lights on the porches of other cabins, and in those cabins were my uncle's family, and my grandfather's friends and his brother and his brother's daughters. For a month each summer, all those people and others gathered at this place, occupying virtually all the rentals. I don't know how they took the time away from work; no one has that kind of time now.

Even the days and nights lasted longer. Every night was vast and free and unboundaried for the kids, and for the teenagers, vaster and freer and probably as truly erotic as anything would ever be again, erotic being something entirely different from a hard sexual blast. After dinner, they gathered in a shack down a dirt road and played records—first with the lights on, later with the lights out, returning to their parents with their lips swollen around magnificence they could never confide, knowing, as they did, that their parents had never experienced anything similar, which is as true now for my own kids with me as it was with me and my parents then. I have no idea what they feel.

As a kid, even one of the older supervisory kids, I knew I had it good and wasn't as eager as some of my cousins or the daughters of my parents' friends to give that up. Until I was twelve, I ran crazy with the little ones, jumping out of rowboats, jumping off piers, jumping off rocks higher than first stories, throwing mud clots at each other, washing the mud off at the hoses and climbing over the fence to jump into what was then a truly luxe accoutrement, an outdoor pool. Why our parents never stopped us from jumping off a diving board into a pool at night, I have no idea. There were no lights around that pool, except for a single tiny bulb above the door of a little changing house with the filters inside it. By rights, at least six of the cousins and friends should have been paralyzed.

By my thirteenth summer, I was a babysitter, miserably betwixt. By my fourteenth and last summer at that place, I was too old for any of it, or if I was not, I felt I had to be.

On the sticky days, freshened by the wind impossibly high up in the tops of the pines, I sat on the porch and read. Or I read under the trees, my long legs tucked under me. I hated the feeling of the earth on my Johnson's-baby-oiled skin and imagined ants crawling up the legs of my tight cutoff jeans, but I knew it looked good. There was nothing I would not suffer, even rolling my hair on cored cans that had held concentrated orange juice, to look as close to good as possible.

"Do you read all the time?" the boy asked me. I hadn't seen him coming, hadn't heard the motor of his mower cut off. For the first and only time in my life, I literally fell over, hitting my head on a sharp pebble in a way that formed a spot that remained tender well into the school year, and which I, the seventies equivalent of an emotional cutter, used to rub on purpose to make myself cry. The book I was reading was one I'd found under the pot holders, where my mother kept the things I was too young to consume. I had no idea that this was "literature." I knew it was a good story. It was about a woman who left her husband for a cavalry soldier, a long time ago in Russia. Already, I could tell things weren't going to go well for them.

"No," I said.

"Do you like to go swimming?" he asked. "You can go swimming in the pool. I'll go swimming with you."

These things were all too much to take in together. I liked to swim and I ached for this boy as much as Anna in the novel ached for her soldier, even though I suppose I was naive then and didn't know exactly what the nature of such an abdominal ache, a near queasiness, was. At least entirely. To go swimming with this boy would mean to walk around in front of him in my decorous two-piece swimsuit made of some horrifying stretchy waffle cloth. But that wasn't the problem. It would mean that I would have to go change into that swimsuit, which would mean that wherever he was, changing into his swimsuit, he would know that at some point, perhaps at the same moment as he, I would have all my clothes off.

That much, I wasn't sure I could manage emotionally.

"No," I said. "I'll stay here."

"Why? Can't you swim?"

"I can swim. I'm a good swimmer. You've seen me swim, at night, when...when I was a kid."

"What then?"

I got up and dusted all the anthill dust off my rear and put my finger in the book and pretended to be someone else other than the piercingly, excruciatingly self-conscious girl I was—and still am now, forty years later.

Without telling the boy whether I was walking away from him in annoyance or going to change, I went into the house and, through the cheap, nearly transparent curtains of our cabin, watched him walk up the hill to his grandparents' house. Within minutes he was diving and dipping in the pool, his blond hair curling. Wrapped in two towels, I sort of sidled down there. It took me an hour to finally get wet, but soon we were horsing around in that kind of rough foreplay that really is play, joined by two of my friends and then his younger cousin—or was it his brother?—who was probably, in modern terms, a cuter boy.

For me, there was no other boy.

There hadn't been any other boy since I first saw him, probably when I was eleven years old.

And there wouldn't be, at least in that way of that novel, for ten years—and in some very real sense, beyond.

Later that night, when I agreed to meet him under the light of that humming little house where people changed into their swimsuits—how could they do that?—I honestly didn't know if he would kiss me. No one had ever kissed me. I didn't even know if I would be "good at it." All my friends had certifiably made out, some even while lying down, some even while lying on a bed. "Making out," at least in my neighborhood, didn't mean then what it does now; but it meant a whole universe beyond all the physical thrills I'd ever known—which amounted to Danny Pepper's hand on the small of my back at the Friday night mixer. I do know that when the blue-eyed boy pressed me against the wall and brought my whole body to symphonic life from the mouth down, sliding his hands down my back, along my sides, under my arms without ever quite touching my breasts, leaving me with a literal mark on my abdomen the shape of his belt buckle, a mark I cherished and checked so often that my mother finally asked me about it, it was evident I had never been born to want to do anything else and I would never for an hour, not for decades, think about anything else again without thinking about that first time.

Was he my boyfriend? Afterward? I didn't know enough to wonder.

That we would kiss, that night and every night for the three weeks left in the month, was never in question. That this would entail any other kind of contract was something I never dared to bring up. How could I ask for more? He was my first one. He was right there, his eyes always on me. He smelled like the water and Aramis and the pine tops and the white flowers in the hedge and his eyes were blue as a water-made pebble. If he'd done more to me at that moment, I might have pushed him away.

I doubt it.

For the rest of the time I knew him—although I would see him only two more times, once under nearly (literally) military supervision, once, ludicrously, two hours after I'd had four teeth pulled—I would think of him. I think of him now. I unravel and knit up again those hours at the pool house (and later in the woods, and across the lake, on a deserted little spit of beach, where only the T-shirt over my bathing suit separated his hot skin from mine).

And I wish we had done more.

It's not that I would now hope that my own daughter, who is the same age I was then, would do more than have a sweet kiss. As a mother, I would find that repugnant, awful. What we did was perfect. Although he was eighteen and had cared for other girls, he was also innocent. I could tell that. Why I wished that we had done more, done everything, was because of what later happened to him—and so to me.

That first night, when he gave me a moment to breathe, he asked my age and I said I was fifteen. I said I had a learner's permit. Later he began to ask me about the particulars of my drivers' ed class and I had to confess my real age. I was horrified and nearly stuck together inside with my fear that he would push me away, wipe away the taste of my mouth.

He didn't.

I'm pretty sure now he'd always known.

I wrote him a hundred letters after the summer ended.

He was a boy, although a lovely, romantic boy, and he wrote only three to me—each of them just a few lines. When the time came, I went to high school, and a couple of years later, there were other boys. Still, whenever an envelope came embossed with his sweet, curiously girlish cursive, all thoughts of those other boys fell away. With other boys, I had done many more and various make-out things, none of which felt as glorious as those nights under the yellow light at the fishing resort. Maybe I went further and further, hoping they would make me feel that way.

And how I treasured those letters—that is, when I could get to them before my mother did. The boy was older. The fact that I was sixteen and then seventeen, and already two years into college by then, mattered to him not at all. Despite how often I wrote and asked him to send his letters to my dorm and then the sordid apartment I shared with a couple of girls and a boy who dressed better than all three of us, he never did; he seemed to locate me at my childhood home.

There my mother thought it was her right not only to possess but to read those letters: I didn't know until I overheard her. I was home on a weekend and heard her quoting from those letters to the guy who rented a store downstairs from our apartment—quoting from them disdainfully, telling the fellow how the boy and I would never be alone together again, despite his having been lewd and rude enough to suggest that. This was an invasion that left me feeling like a human being among aliens: I never really admitted to myself that my mother, meddlesome as she was, would do such a thing.

She would later defend her reasons to my stunned-deaf ears: The boy was then a hardened man. I was still, at least to her way of thinking, a girl.

The war in Vietnam was at that time dragging to an inglorious end. Not a fraction as political as I would become, even I knew that this page of our country's behavior was stained with nastier things even than young blood. When the boy wrote to me that he had stopped college and the dumb job he'd taken working with his mother's new husband and had enlisted in the Marines, I was struck mad. How could he do such a thing? With everything but the most meaningless brute days already finished? I was distraught. But I couldn't call him; I didn't know his camp address yet and wouldn't call his house. His parents had been divorced when divorce was still a novelty. The new stepfather—whom the boy always referred to as "Chuckles"—was where I put the blame for the stupidity. The boy had run from a rut into a trap. Instead, I tried to find that place on my abdomen where his belt buckle had branded me nearly four years before, but I couldn't and I pressed and pressed until my own fingers hurt me so badly I finally could cry.

For months I wouldn't speak to my mother. My mother kept on insisting she had her reasons for trying to derail the relationship: It was already an antique. I was headed someplace. He was just a soldier.

She apologized.

For months I would not hear her.

I loved my mother wildly, and I would regret a thousand other things I said only two years later, when she died young. But what I said to her the first day that I learned about her stealing my letters is something I never regretted. I still don't. I think she understood the lurid insult of not only violating but also broadcasting her child's life. I think she understood that she did not own me. Still, she'd gone so far that admitting that would have divested her of some cloak of moral rectitude, leaving her flawed and afraid.

Back then, I had a purse made by one of my artsy girlfriends, sewn with thongs from cheap leatherette and festooned with the fringes of the revolution. In the dark hyacinth-blue lining, I slit a place between the skin of the purse and the lining, a pocket no one could see, and I padded it with his letters, in their envelopes, in date order. I was overjoyed when finally he did write to me at college, a birthday card from a camp in California that said, "You're eighteen. Now [he quoted the old John Sebastian song 'Younger Girl'] they'd call us right for each other." I think I believed that he would come home and somehow, despite the intervening years, despite that he was a Navy SEAL and I was a bone-deep pacifist, I would be his.

Before he left for overseas, my grandparents, headed for a visit with friends in San Francisco (my grandparents were married when my grandfather was seventeen and she was fourteen), took pity on me. They drove out of their way, in their big maroon Bonneville, to bring me to see the boy. We spent an hour kissing, pressed against the hot concrete wall of a barracks, while my grandparents hovered nearby and other soldiers said things. I flew home alone. A few weeks later he came through my hometown, just days before he left. I'd had surgery on my mouth, and he couldn't kiss me at all. My mother allowed me to go out with him to a nearby restaurant, but she called the place five times while we were there. And then we said goodbye.

The striped airmail letters came, slender things with their burden of stamps, from places with beautiful, clipped-sounding names, each month for a year.

Then they stopped.

I had a boyfriend at home who might as well have been a hamster, for all the emotion he evoked from me then. I checked the mailbox morning and night. I lost my appetite and my zest for school. The war had ended late in the spring. I came home for the summer and my mother was appalled at the way I looked. With more bravado than zest, she said, "I'm sure he's fine. I'm sure he found some…woman." She said, "You're lucky I didn't show those letters to your father. He'd have burned them."

I said, "You're lucky I don't smother you in your sleep when you stole what was mine."

Then we both began to cry. She was beautiful and gaunt, already sick, although we would not know that for months, and I was horrified. As it turned out, I needed her desperately in the weeks to come: I found out the end of this story, or almost the end, which you must already know if you have read this far, when I found out from his cousin or brother why the letters stopped.

I didn't believe him.

I truly thought, or hoped or fantasized, that he had actually found some woman and was hiding under the ruse of a warrior's death. I thought he was lost, holed up in a cave like those soldiers from World War II. A prison camp. AWOL. An error, because he had an ordinary surname, Johnstone.

So one day, I called the house where the boy had grown up. His mother, who was very young and had a name that didn't seem suitable to a mother—something like Stacey or Kim—knew who I was and was harsh, or so I thought then, and brief with me, wanting only to get away from any voice, to get off the telephone. Now I have five sons of my own. And I know that if I were to choose to survive any of them who died before me, a reminder of them sweet and beautiful and young and in love for the first time would be acid in my mouth.

I did say, "I was his friend. My name is Jackie."

"He had your picture with the things they sent me," she said. "Do you want it?"

I said no. I said I was sorry. But I was sorry for myself: his mother wasn't real to me.

Alone, on the fire escape, although I am no drinker now and wasn't then, I drank a bottle of red wine and smoked a pack of Marlboros. I spent the next day throwing up. Then I did the whole thing over again.

A couple of months later, my boyfriend and I were playing a board game in the living room in the apartment of friends—who were in graduate school in a state far south of where he and I lived, who were one of those baby couples there seemed to be more of then, married and nested at the age of twenty-one—when there was a quiet burglary in the kitchen. The thief simply walked in the open back door and took a joint, a little plastic radio, a half-filled bottle of vodka. Whoever it was also took my purse with the hippie fringe— along with all the letters that were still in the lining.

Some years later, I moved back to Chicago. I married a guy I'd never known growing up, although we'd rarely been more than ten miles apart, and I took a job as a low, low-level editor on a city magazine. Gradually I moved up. I became a section editor. We had a baby boy; we adopted another baby boy. Late one Friday afternoon, I let a woman who worked with me talk me into driving up to central Wisconsin—an eight-hour round-trip—to a thrift shop where, legend had it, used fur coats could be had for forty dollars. We arrived as the store was closing, talking the person who ran it into letting us come in just for fifteen minutes.

My coworker was joyously modeling a full-length raccoon, with only one gaping hole in the armpit, when I saw the purse in the window. Brown suede. Fringe and a long strap.

"How much is that purse?" I asked.

"The little Woodstock-y purse?" the girl asked.

"Whatever it is," I said. "Can you get it out of the window?"

"Sure," she said.

"How much?" I asked, not looking at it, holding it in my hand, away from my body.

"Say, three dollars."

All the long way home, I kept it clutched in the folded paper sack. I waited until my sons were bathed and asleep and my husband deep in his Civil War history book. I didn't want to open it and thought I might wait forever, because every girl I knew had a purse just like it. But finally, I shook it out of the paper sack all at once and held it to my face, inhaling the smell of old pocket change and some ancient cologne. With one fingernail, I felt for the slit I had cut with my nail scissors.

They were all there, so thin by their nature and so compressed by time that they barely made a noticeable bulge. And yet, they were weighty. On their own, in that dark room where I sat alone, they compressed time indeed—not that time had ever erased the boy or his smell or the shape of his hands, small for a guy, not bigger than my own, though for a woman, my hands are very big. I slept in my kids' room that night, with the purse cuddled under my rib cage, as my son slept with his rag doll. In the morning, I slipped the purse into my glass-fronted bookcase, between two heavy dictionaries. I can see it there now.

I didn't read them.

For years I thought about this, about writing down how I received them and lost them and received them again, because it's a strange tale. Now I have, and I think I'll fold this story in with the letters inside that purse. There's only a small chance that I'll share them before I die, and I can't see why I would—except if it were to be for a huge school project or with a grandchild. I can't imagine wanting to let anyone else see his letters for anything less than a master's thesis. Yet, I wouldn't mind someone finding them when I am dead. There are things I own that I would want destroyed before I die, but not these letters. I would want my children to know that this was something that mattered, that lasted one month and twenty years. These letters. They're not cute and they're not really funny and they're not really history—although I suspect my someday grown kids would find them all that and quaint, as well. What they comprise is a holy relic of something they've probably never been able to imagine me being—a girl purely in love and in love purely, white-hot as snow.

It's hard for me to believe that I was that girl once, myself.

Sometimes I think they don't make guiltless girls and gallant boys that way anymore. Sometimes I think that's just as well.

# When It Was All Brand-New

## Rebecca Walker

I met my first crush while riding a red ten-speed bicycle my grand-mother bought for me at Sears. I was twelve years old, in the sixth grade and new in town. Town being hilly, sunny San Francisco, my new place in the world after my parents' divorce. I was wearing jeans with red satin stripes down the side that my stepmother had picked up for me at a little store called Bloomingdale's. My forest-green T-shirt still had my name tag sewn on the label from summer camp.

Michael was not so tall, but dark and very handsome. He had full lips and almond-shaped eyes and jet-black hair, which I eventually liked to run my fingers through. He had a few pimples, but for the most part his skin was smooth, and the most delicious shade of brown. He took to wearing polo shirts by Ralph Lauren and Levi's 501 jeans. Of course, as these things often go, Michael was older. Like maybe five years older. Which is a lot of years when you're in the sixth grade.

But he was gorgeous. When I met him, I swear his phero-mones made me drunk with attraction. He didn't have to say much, because I was in the sixth grade. Dreams were the point, not words. Dreams of wearing his football jersey to school, dreams of us talk-ing to each other on the phone all night long, dreams of long make-out sessions in places I couldn't yet imagine, dreams of bragging to other girls that he was my boyfriend. Dreams he would like me, just one iota.

We met on a sunny Saturday morning. He was riding his bike through the neighborhood, and he stopped and asked my name. He looked at me with interest, amusement and, I think, a tiny bit of desire. A few days later, he stood up for me against a few neigh-borhood bullies who tried to steal my bike. Then he showed me the secret way to the Peace Pagoda in Japantown, which was on the other side of a six-lane boulevard from my house. There was a spot you could cross easily without being run over by cars speeding on their way downtown. It was fantastic.

Eventually he told me I was cute, and that he liked my curly hair and big smile.

"I haven't seen you in the neighborhood much," he said that first day. "Did you just move here?"

"I'm from New York," I said proudly, putting my kick-stand down.

He was visibly impressed. He had never left San Francisco and immediately asked endless questions about my other city. Did peo-ple really beat you up all the time? What was the music like? Were the streets really dirty? And what about the subway? Did I ride it, like, all the time? Was graffiti painted all over the sides? I answered his questions one by one, trying to stay calm.

"Um, no, I mean, I never got beat up."

"I used to ride the subways with my dad to his office. They are really hot in the summertime, and you just sweat and sweat and wait to get back to air-conditioning. But I guess there is a lot of graffiti."

Being a New Yorker, I hadn't noticed.

"We get the same music as here, but it, like, gets here later. At least that's what I think. I like that song by Lisa Lisa, 'I Wonder if I Take You Home,' but I haven't heard it on the radio here at all."

He nodded his head, taking it all in, re-visioning the New York of his imagination. We were sitting on a cement bench across from a row of fir trees. St. Mary's Cathedral dominated our makeshift refuge from a few blocks up. Michael was on his way to work, cleaning tables in the dining room of a home for senior citizens.

I felt special sitting next to him, singled out. He could talk to any girl, or at least that's what I thought then, but he had chosen me. And I know I already said this and you, dear reader, should expect to hear it again, but it wasn't just that he had chosen me. It was also that I already, almost instantly, liked being so close I could smell him; it was like breathing in the aroma of freshly baked bread on the sidewalk in front of the best bakery in town.

Maybe it was just Tide detergent, but all I wanted to do after we met in the neighborhood and he stuck up for me and asked my name and taught me how to get to the Peace Pagoda where I could ride my bike on the smooth concrete, was be next to him so I could inhale his, his, whatever that was. The urge was so strong that if we were in another culture, where girls and boys get married at fourteen and have kids and live with their parents and grandparents their whole lives, I'm sure Michael and I would have had ten kids. That's how intense the pheromones were. It was bigger than attraction, this crush. It was genetic. Our genes wanted to come together to make a baby.

Which was why I ended up going to Planned Parenthood and getting a prescription for the Pill six months after we met. I was afraid of those pheromones, and my budding desire. But I'm getting ahead of myself.

At some point in our courtship—which involved riding around the neighborhood, noticing each other on our bikes and then stopping and talking about other kids we knew, New York and rap music—I noticed Michael's body. He played football. His thighs were very shapely and, as I remember now, quite erotic. Certainly I didn't think that then. But I certainly had the jolt of the way they looked in his pants. I absolutely wondered about what else was in his pants.

I was very precocious, and he was very handsome, in the jock kind of way that was so popular. (He had a Members Only jacket!) As already stated, I also really, really liked him, which meant, among other things, that I got completely turned around, flushed red and started to sweat when I saw him. It also meant I wanted him to keep liking me. And that, I figured, had something to do with kissing. But here's the thing: I knew there was no way he was going to kiss a sixth grader. Like, no way. He was in high school. He was a football player, with real live cheerleaders shaking pom-poms during his games.

So I lied about my age. I told him I was fourteen. I have no idea if he believed me. If I were to see him now, if we were to have lunch, I would ask him. Did you really believe I was fourteen? If he did, I was way more precocious than I remember, because it was quite a stretch, saying I was fourteen, a seriously gutsy move. But it did the trick; it was the magic key to the seemingly impenetrable lock. Michael became my boyfriend. First came the crush, then something more.

Kissing became our full-time obsession. If we weren't making out in front of the Laundromat in our neighborhood, on the sofa in the small apartment I lived in with my mother, or in the basement of his house, we were talking about it on the phone or, at least I was, imagining when it was to occur again. The kissing. Which was unbelievable. And if we were some place private, the kissing would happen lying on top of each other and he would wrap his arms around me and we would kiss and then I would bury my nose in his armpit and inhale.

I'm older now, so a kiss is great and fireworks sometimes go off and a kiss can take you all kinds of places you don't expect, but there's nothing like those first kisses, the ones where you feel you're going to fall inside the other person, when you get dizzy and forget who you are. When Michael and I kissed, every thought I had, every synapse set to connect, declined to fire. All I knew was his butterflying tongue inside of my mouth, and when we came up for air, I almost fell over because my brain had lost communication with my body.

We listened to Michael Jackson on my record player. We went to see *Purple Rain*. By the time he found out my real age—a jealous girl from his school ratted me out—it was too late. He was my boyfriend. The crush was in full bloom.

We were having sex.

Sex was exciting, and oh, so intimate. Then, even though I took my little white Pill religiously, I became pregnant, and Michael came with me to have an abortion, which was awful and a huge relief. Awful because I was too young to process what was happening, and a relief because I had no idea what it all meant in the big picture—only that I was way too young to have a baby.

What can I say? It was a different time. My friends and I smoked pot, and our parents let us stay out in the neighborhood after dark. It wasn't like today. Parents didn't hover in metaphoric helicopters to make sure of our whereabouts, or scrutinize peanut butter labels for corn syrup. And there was the whole pheromone thing, which isn't an excuse. I swear.

Michael and I broke up a year or so after that, when I met another guy with equally strong pheromonal activity. But we remained friends, and it was always good to see him. Whenever I visited San Francisco years later, I called him and we had lunch or met up at a club or concert. We always flirted with each other a little bit, because we knew each other's sexual secrets. We made them.

No matter whom I was dating or what I was doing, Michael represented something to me—a time I could never recapture. Michael reminded me of when it was all brand-new, and anything was possible. He reminded me of the time before relationships came to follow a known pattern, a particular path. When a romantic choice didn't have to be run through the filters of where the person lived or what type of family they came from.

Fast-forward ten years to a phone call from another ex. She and Michael had bonded around their love for music and, I optimistically like to think, me. Long after we broke up, they remained friends and hung out together when she visited San Francisco.

She called my cell. I was working on a book. Distracted. She told me Michael had a brain tumor. He was depressed. Confused. He couldn't remember people or places. But he remembered me, and she thought seeing me would be good for him, and maybe for me. Would I go to the hospital? I snapped to attention. I scrawled the address on a piece of paper. Michael had what? I was stunned.

I'm not sure if you will understand this, dear reader, but I went into a kind of shock when I got this news. Brain tumors are not supposed to happen to crushes that turn into first loves. First loves are supposed to live forever, to die within a month of your own death, to inhabit some miraculous imaginary space full of hazy atmospheric images and twinges of nostalgia. Hospitals and brain surgery don't fit into the picture at all. Not one bit.

I went, first, into denial. I ended the call with a snap shut of my cell and returned immediately to work. Then I cleaned my house from top to bottom and tried not to think of Michael lying in an operating room somewhere, having his skull sawed open and his brain penetrated by a tiny scalpel. I kept my mind on our kisses, and I sent all the love and all the hope I had through the ether of time and space. I didn't contact him directly, and I didn't call his mother or his sister. I didn't go visit the house where I had spent so many hours, days and nights. I put the piece of information in a little space in my mind and kept it there—separate from everything else.

I've never told anyone this, and I still feel awful about it, but to this day I have not seen or talked to Michael. I don't know if he is still alive. I can't. It is too much. In addition to having awful, ridiculous thoughts like *Are brain tumors contagious?*, I've thought a lot about my small son. What if Michael's bad luck rubbed off right when things in my own life were going well? Dear reader, I feel I am going to burn in hell for even writing such words.

But really I know it's not any of those things, because I've visited and cared for friends in far worse shape than Michael. It's just that even though illness and death are the things life is made of,

I am, selfishly, unable to give Michael up. Not the Michael of right now, but the Michael I remember. He was always older, and stronger. He always looked at me with teenage love in his eyes, even when we were in our thirties. He always took my side, had my back and laughed at my lame attempts at making jokes. He was always alive. Clear. Himself.

I wasn't ready to meet another Michael. I'm still not, and even though others may disagree, I'm not sure it's such a bad thing. There are certain moments in life that should be remembered, encased in the magic of another time and space, and left alone. I can only hope Michael understands. I selfishly think he does. After all, it's the only way we can still meet there, in that magical space when it was all brand-new.

# A Bruise for Every Broken Heart

## Kerry Cohen

In my early twenties, I had a habit of getting a tattoo after a breakup. The first was during college, after my first real love. His name was Eli, and with typical first-love naïveté, I had believed we would wind up married. Before him I had thrown myself at boys—too many boys—wanting their attention to my body to mean something more than it ever did. Eli was the first one who stayed. He could be cruel to me and easily annoyed, but his mother was the mother I thought I had always wanted. I loved her, in some ways more than I loved him. She was earthy, thoughtful, generous, and she liked having me around. I didn't want to lose Eli, because I didn't want to lose his mom. But also, I couldn't imagine that someone would finally love me and then leave. I was still virginal in this way when it came to breakups.

When our relationship ended, I was devastated. I lay on my bed, hollow and hurting, unable to cry. I was sure I was the only one who had ever felt this way and so deeply. I held the phone against my ear well into the night, going over and over the relationship with my friends. I told them all the things you believe when you've been dumped: I would always feel this way, I wasn't worth loving, and no one would ever love me again. One day, sitting in my kitchen with a friend, going over the same terrain again, my friend, surely exhausted by my relentless sorrow, suggested we get tattoos. This was the early nineties, when tattoos were hot and relatively new to the mainstream scene. My own mother, always eager to be different, had gotten a tattoo in her forties, when I was ten years old. She had taken me along, and I had watched as a heavyset, bearded man in a clean white T-shirt pressed the buzzing needle into her behind. I had studied her face, concerned by her wincing. Afterward she'd showed it to me: a lavender iris, her favorite flower. It was a delicate little thing, placed secretly where no one but she and a lover would see. I knew that my father was in the process of leaving her. He had been having an affair for years, and the tattoo—I sensed even then from my mother's determination—was my mother's way of inflicting something on herself, something both painful and lovely, something that was all hers.

My mother and I were similar in many ways. We both wrestled with the same harsh whispers, both desperately wanted to be loved. But while she held on to this affinity for secretiveness, held herself back—from men, from me—as I grew through my girlhood, I did the opposite. I charged forward. I reached for people, for men, trying to make them mine. And so, I didn't want my tattoo to be hidden like my mother's. I wanted mine out in the open, where everyone could see it. I thought that a tattoo was sexy because everyone could see that you opted for pain, that you chose to hurt yourself. I thought a tattoo was commanding and powerful because it meant you were hurting yourself before someone else hurt you. To me, a tattoo was proof of something, a suggestion of hidden things.

In the week before my friend and I went to see her friend's brother, who had a start-up tattoo operation out of his dorm, I gave myself what I called pain therapy. While my friend spent this week researching pictures for her tattoo, I was busy using an Epilady to see how much pain I could stand. I found I could stand a lot. We drove to Rhode Island from our college town in Massachusetts. The friend's brother injected an amateur picture of a blue thunderbird, a stereotypical Native American symbol, that I had picked quickly and without much thought before we left. I didn't waste time thinking about what little connection I had to the symbol. Sure, I studied Native American literature. Sure, I liked the way it looked, bright blue and conspicuous on my shoulder blade. But beneath that tattoo I was just a privileged Jewish girl from Jersey with no real connection to the symbol I was claiming for myself. It didn't hurt very much, not as much as the Epilady, and that was that. I had my first tattoo.

It was summer then, and as I walked across campus, the thunderbird visible through tank top straps, I felt my life coming back. I passed guys. There were more guys! How had I forgotten? I smiled seductively, hoping they would see the tattoo. And soon, I was back at it, searching for the next boy who could make me feel whole.

I got my second tattoo when my next relationship ended. This one had been with a boy I loved, a musician whose mind was always on compositions and riffs. He smoked pot just about every day and sat always with his guitar on his lap like a shield. We had come together in a rush of lust; then, to my surprise and delight, he stayed. Over time, though, I wanted more from our relationship, and predictably, he wanted less. We moved together across country after college, and bored, sad, never fulfilled, I cheated on him with someone else. When we broke up, I crawled into bed once more and couldn't get out for days. The emptiness felt like poison. The same friend with whom I'd gotten that first ugly tattoo, who had also moved across the country, quickly suggested we get another one, and, anxious for relief, I went with her to a guy named Diamond. This time I got an anklet. I picked out the pattern right there in Diamond's shop. It was a pretty design that I found out later was Celtic and that, like the thunderbird, had nothing to do with me. I was just happy that men would see it above my flip-flops and whenever I wore short skirts.

A few months later, after yet another series of short-lived affairs, after more yearning and reaching with each and every boy I invited into my bed, I got my third tattoo. I was sure by now that I was the only one who felt as I did, sure that I was the only girl who took each breakup as proof of her inability to be loved, sure that I was the only one with whom no boy ever wanted to stay. The shame felt tremendous, and I knew others could see it in that first tattoo on my back, in its hurried, hastily drawn shape. It was so damn ugly, so embarrassingly unrelated to me, such a terrible, blatant reminder of my desperation after Eli. I went back to Diamond and had him superimpose a raven over the thunderbird—ravens are black and I needed something black to cover the blue of the first bird. It didn't completely work. You could still see that there was something beneath the raven, but at least you couldn't make out what.

I got the fourth and final tattoo after my last breakup, this time with a boy I didn't actually love but stayed with because I identified with his sadness, until finally I managed to leave. By this time it was just habit to get a tattoo. Get a broken heart, stitch something onto my body. It no longer made me feel sexy or in control. It was simply what I did. I got a haircut, slept with someone new and got a tattoo—my breakup triad. Perhaps because I was acting from halfheartedness, this tattoo was the ugliest, stupidest one yet—a bear on my shoulder. I still wanted people to see it, still frantically wanted people to believe that this bear represented me—wise, strong, powerful and feminine—but the picture looked cuddly and worn, like a beat-up teddy bear from childhood.

Many years later, after more self-harm with men, more giving my body away, I finally began the process of change. This process was achingly slow. Friends beat their heads against walls. "Hold back," they'd tell me for the 378th time. "Don't give yourself away so easily. Make him work for it." I saw my tattoos in the mirror as I dressed, night after night after night, for another evening on the town. They were so ugly, but I was also used to them. They were just these parts of me, faded now, not so bright and eye-catching, but still there.

Eventually, I met the man I would marry. He was a good man—kind and funny. He was a friend first, which meant the passion was gentle and serene, so different from the sharp claws passion had always held for me in the past. During our engagement, I went to a specialist to try to get that bear removed. I wished I could get rid of all my tattoos, but it was extremely costly—over one hundred dollars per session—and also, I soon learned, extremely painful, so I settled on just the bear. The procedure went like this: the nice woman put on protective glasses, gave me a pair to wear, and then held a laser gun against the bear, aimed and pulled the "trigger" as if she were at a shooting gallery. With each clicking sound it felt as though she were stabbing me with a knife covered in hot sauce. I gritted my teeth through the two minutes, trying not to yell out, and then I left with a prescription antibiotic to help it heal. The bear remained sore and oozed for a good four to five days each time. Four weeks later the tattoo was completely healed, but always it was still there—slightly faded since the last time, but never enough. After four sessions, though, I was out of money.

My husband-to-be made jokes. "It's bear-ly there anymore. I can bear-ly see it." Did it matter, really, that I couldn't make them go away? Maybe it didn't. Maybe—as tattoos tend to go— they were a permanent part of me, something I should learn to accept.

The other day, I stepped from the shower, and just as I wrapped a towel around myself, my two-year-old son pushed open the door, slamming it into the back wall.

"Hi, Mommy," he said.

"Hi there, monkey," I replied.

He moved closer, a funny look on his face. After a moment I understood what he was looking at.

"What dat?" he asked, pointing to the raven on my shoulder blade.

"That's Mommy's bird," I told him.

He stared a moment longer. "What dat?" he asked, unsatisfied with my first answer.

"It's a tattoo of a bird," I told him. "Mommy got it when she was young and not making very good choices." I could have gone on, but I stopped myself, reminding myself he was only two.

"What doing?" he asked, smiling.

"It's just sitting there," I said, "perched on Mommy's shoulder."

He nodded. "Okay, Mommy."

Okay.

# Sweet Nothings

## Robert Wilder

Years before: Mrs. Calvert, the younger and second wife of my
father's friend Bob, pressed close on the couch in our Point Lookout living room, saying she had something to teach me. It was a
summer night and I was six or seven, eight tops. She looked like
a combination of Raquel Welch and Ann-Margret and, later I realized, Tina Louise (one of my future television fantasies).

"Someday, a girl will do this," she said in her best Marilyn
Monroe, and blew lightly into my ear and onto the back of my sunburned neck. Alcohol and citrus floated lightly on her breath. Her
ginger hair was curled at the ends; her makeup expertly applied.
Pursed red lips. Even for casual parties, the women in my parents'
social group got all dolled up.

"Do you know what this is called?" A tunnel of air grazed my
skin, raising pinpricks of flesh. My tongue lay dry and thick. I
could not speak.

"Sweet nothings," she said, letting the s linger. My skin grew warm like a heated wet suit. I sat perfectly still. I wanted her to stop. I wanted her to keep going (she was the most beautiful woman we knew, after all). I wanted her to...I didn't know what I wanted.

A year before the kiss: that summer was a busy one, the six of us moving into a neglected split-level ranch dividing an acre of verdant lawn almost down the middle. We inherited a swampy pool, walls with cheap wood paneling, worn shag carpeting and stacks of rumors that the previous owners, the Lambs, were what my dad disgustingly referred to as "swingers." There were clues, too. A single light shone on a darker square of brick over the family room fireplace, where, according to neighbors, a screen was hung for adult films and, when it wasn't movie night, a naked picture of Mrs. Lamb, the mother who I knew was nothing like my own.

My parents were Catholic and careful people, so all that dark, untidy and funny business was quickly erased soon after we arrived. The six of us Wilders spent the humid summer clearing overgrown brush, building and rebuilding rock walls, spreading layers of mulch to control the weeds and turning the murky pool with its unruly landscaping and dark shadows into a wholly antiseptic experience.

The girl: Liz Thomas. There was something unassuming about those two first names joined casually together, and the soft endings of each word made saying her name aloud sound almost like Mrs. Calvert's sweet nothings. But she was something: petite, quick to smile (showing only a row of straight white upper teeth) and a Dorothy Hamill haircut, only lighter and shorter.

My eyes followed her on the playground with Martha or in the hallway with Bettina and I thought she was the prettiest girl at Greens Farms Elementary. Prettier than Stephanie Baker, Jennifer Franklin, even Kathy Cullen. There was something else, too, something that most of us lost as we ventured into that overgrown thicket of adolescence, a kindness and openness that didn't waver no matter who she was talking to—awkward student, dull teacher or Mr. Betts, the imposing custodian. Liz and Martha would often ride by and stop at my house on their way to Kathy Charlton's or to the new tire swing park at Greens Farms. I felt no awkwardness with Martha, but when Liz showed up, my hands appeared oversize and my tongue swelled. I tried holding in my stomach but that restricted my air flow, so I became breathy telling her the score of the basketball game I was playing with my brother Tom. Liz made me nervous but she never let on that she knew (if she noticed). There was nothing or no one in the world I felt more affection toward and I thought I was keeping it my great secret until one night when Martha rolled by on her bike, alone.

"Liz likes you," Martha said, still straddling her beat-up bike.

I scowled at her. Surely she was extracting revenge for the times Spoon (our nickname for my brother Rich) had dumped that yellow ten-speed into the deep end of the pool.

"Just thought you should know. Maybe you could call her or something."

Then I watched her leave me alone in front of my garage, ride up my steep and short driveway, and hang a right toward her home on Morningside Drive. I stood there, her information feeling more like a punch in the gut I hadn't bothered to suck in than being awarded the grand prize on a game show. I wanted to call Liz. I wish I didn't know. I wanted to tell someone. I wanted no one to know (and prayed Martha didn't say anything to anyone else). I didn't know what I wanted.

The year: 1978. There is no way to tell now why we chose my house for the party. Maybe because it was close to Greens Farms and offered a family room that was on a lower level from the places my father sipped Beefeater Gibsons and my mother Diet 7UP after giving up drinking before the move. (My parents were nothing if not efficient. Their deal: my mother would quit drinking if there were to be no more children. A fair trade, according to my dad.) Or maybe it was because the cutest boy in the school, Micu Oprea, a future Versace model and low-budget movie star, gave it his blessing or more likely volunteered for me.

No matter how it came about, everyone was there: my neighbor Kathy Charlton, the other Kathy (Cullen), Micu, Will Vail, Martha, Tim Pape, kids I can't recall and Liz Thomas. Kathy Charlton carried over her older sister's copy of *Saturday Night Fever*—the other white album. I'd moved accompanied with the one by the Beatles and soon learned to understand the importance of the LP with the Bee Gees. From my guitar gently weeping alone in Point Lookout to dreaming of asking "How deep is your love?" to Liz. Kathy carefully removed the vinyl disc from its sleeve. I lay it on my parents' RCA turntable and switched the silver knob to B, channeling the music to the downstairs speakers only.

After my parents said an obligatory hello and I slid closed the door we never closed, the ten of us were separated from the parental world above, yet dangerously near to that exit hatch of a sliding glass door behind us that would lead, in a few years, to more adult pursuits. Filled with an excited terror, I found it difficult to control my tremors. Of all the players involved, in my mind, I was still the least savory. Micu was every girl's dream (probably some boys', as well) and Will Vail, the mayor of our fifth grade class the year before, was bold, brash, and often confirmed what I feared inside. He made fun of the bad haircut I numbly accepted at Mario & Mike's, asked me if I got my pants at Barker's *(What does the Barker's bird say? Cheap! Cheap!)* and poked me in the stomach roll I still carried with me from Point Lookout, singing "chubsy ubsy" in a cartoon lilt.

Earlier in the day, I had auditioned a variety of bottles, starting with my dad's Rolling Rock (too heavy), a Smirnoff fifth (too asymmetrical), and had finally settled on my mother's two-liter Diet 7UP plastic job, which, while running the risk of not staying in one place, rotated enough to allow for a variety of givers and receivers. Trying to get the feel of the friction of plastic on shag, I had practiced using different levels of force and varied wrist flicks. I was self-aware enough to know I needed home court advantage.

Having older sisters well versed in these types of games, Micu had us sit boy/girl on the balding orange shag rug. Dread and excitement wound their way through my veins like entangled vipers. Everything about my inclusion in this ritual was wrong: ruler-straight bangs across my forehead, my two extra chins, awkward apparel. And the room: shag that was clown-wig orange with bald spots as large as Frisbees and walls made of thin wood paneling that had started to pull away from the Sheetrock, so you could spot the seams. Behind our circle of teens was a half-moon bar with elbow padding that matched the carpet and with a base that mirrored the faux wood of the walls. All this to say that these people didn't belong in that room and I didn't belong with these people.

And there was the girl who it all depended on: Liz Thomas. The cutest haircut. Ears like small shells, smile refreshing itself every few minutes, every bit of her sitting right across from me. She seemed more excited than nervous when Micu kissed her, offering something clever and rehearsed as he did with every girl. If he landed on a boy, he'd say, "I'm sorry but you're just not my type" and we'd all hysterically laugh. I rubbed my palms on my pants, believing that if I said the same sort of thing, I'd be asked to leave my own home. Since I'd moved, I'd seen that for a boy like me, wit was important currency and I had consciously tried to develop one. In fifth grade, during a unit on Charles Lindbergh, Mr. Levy videotaped a group of us lip-synching to the song "Lucky Lindy," and I broke free of the simple choreographed moves, wrapped my eyes in finger glasses and can-canned Rockettes style, much to the immediate dismay of my fellow lip-synchers.

But these developing powers were useless in the sexually charged spin-the-bottle territory, especially with Liz present. So I said nothing as dark-haired Kathy Cullen grabbed the bottle and flicked it with slender girl fingers. A few rotations and the container pointed to my left knee. It couldn't have even been a whole second but a jolt of complex feelings overwhelmed me: *kiss me, please don't kiss me, look at me, please look away, I want everyone to like me, I want everyone to get the hell out.*

"Do over," she said, shrugging. Her black hair and pale skin made her look dramatic, sultry even.

"No, no, no," everyone chimed in, hands a-waving. "No way!" someone yelled so loudly it seemed unkind.

"All right, all right." She sighed and moved forward. Her dark eyes never met my dark eyes. Hers clung to the sides of their sockets, while mine were clamped to a bare patch in the shag. In that instant I gave myself strict instructions:

1. Keep your mouth closed (to avoid all the sharp and gooey hazards therein).
2. For God's sake (and your own), don't drool.
3. Don't linger.
4. Don't breathe out (even though I had brushed my teeth like I was visiting a medieval dentist and then swished Listerine around in my mouth until it started to burn holes in my cheeks).

I heard other people exhale when we finished but no one (not even Will Vail) had a chance to comment, because I spun the bottle quickly and it thankfully landed on my neighbor, the other Kathy, like a sister to me.

My focus became more intense, as if I was watching a game of roulette, desperately waiting for my number to hit. Liz was my black seventeen. My mind was clear of all other numbers and I could see her without looking directly, how there was a slight split in her bangs, dividing her chestnut hair almost down the middle. Other rounds and combinations passed by (neighbor Kathy got her long-awaited kiss from Micu) but none of that was important. Even when I had to go upstairs to flip the record after "If I Can't Have You" came to a scratchy end, my mind never left the game. I had only one goal, after all: will the bottle to me, then to her.

Didn't take long and I believed it had something to do with the practicing I had done, but I spun with grand purpose and the green neck settled on her. Our kiss wasn't that lengthy, mashing movie deal, but it wasn't the obligatory peck that I'd received from Kathy Cullen, either. Liz just looked at me and I at her. I half smiled, careful not to grin like a greedy fool. She smiled from under brown bangs. We leaned in. Her lips were soft. Mine felt like balloons, but I hung in there. She didn't pull away quickly and neither did I. If you had been sitting in that circle on that hideous carpet with no padding, you would have noticed a slight something, a tenderness that was mutual and void of the spastic and jerking currents that ran through most of us most of the time. A stillness. After that turn, I picked only Liz and she mostly picked me. Martha's words came true.

The moment: Summer was close enough to feel. School was nearly over, and like all schools, we celebrated the end of the year with an absurd amount of spectacle: carnivals, talent shows and awards ceremonies. The sixth grade had gone on an overnight to Camp Aspetuck, where I (in classic form) had injured myself on the obstacle course and every single member of our class had to inform Liz. We were considered a couple, yet we still hadn't kissed without the aid of a bottle. So we all gathered as a group on Hillandale Lane. Boys on one side. Girls on the other. Even with the division, there was a bipartisan consensus: Liz and I should take a walk.

Each of us was expelled from our cluster of rugby shirts and denim shorts and we met on the corner, near a line of mailboxes. I leaned into her enough to brush her bare arm but neither of us said anything. We passed my house, all lit up in its bowl at the end of the driveway, and I could see the dining room, where my mother would die five years later. Across the street lived a family of girls, the Constantikes, whose lawyer father would keep all the Wilder brothers out of jail at one point (or more) in our future lives. Liz and I still said nothing as we approached Mrs. Flaherty's place. Mrs. Flaherty had lost her husband and spent her days drinking in her floral housecoat, then yelling at us to take our tree fort down, goddammit. She would die that year and there'd be an auction of her possessions to pay the tax man. The Bakers would move in shortly after that, raise two girls, and then Mr. Baker would blow his brains out on the side of the road somewhere down South. Before I left for college, I'd have a torrid love affair with Mrs. Baker that had no way of ending other than badly.

"This is boring," Liz said, a statement she'd later catch hell for from her gaggle of girlfriends.

I answered with a line I'd caught from TV: "I'll make it so it's not boring." I turned to face her. Covered by a dome of leafy shadows, I pressed my lips against hers, holding the back of her head in my hand. Even today there's something magical about that kiss: I got the girl of my dreams and she truly liked me. We kissed only once but then she took my hand in hers and we walked back slowly. Everyone was still alive: the Flahertys, Mr. Baker, Mr. Constantikes, my mother, her mother, Mildred, my aunt Doris, various friends and relatives of friends. None of us were driving yet, so we had yet to endure a string of fatal or near-fatal accidents. The towers still stood tall just an hour south at the edge of Manhattan. Nothing had happened yet something just happened. And now I could hear crickets making time in the freshly trimmed bushes that lined the street in front of our property. There was only me, Liz, our hands pressed together, and our futures waiting on Hillandale Lane.

# The Boy in the White VW Bug

## Ann Hood

The boy in the white VW Bug drove into my life on a summer night in 1970.

Nine months earlier, my brother, Skip, had left for college wearing raspberry Bermuda shorts and a matching polo shirt. He returned that summer a new person in cutoff blue jeans, an army-green T-shirt, with his dirty blond hair hanging in waves to his collarbone. But more than the way he looked had changed about my brother. During his year at college, he had turned from a slightly nerdy, slightly overweight, slide-rule-toting kid into a six-foot-three, handsome man. It was as if a stranger lived in the bedroom next to mine that summer. He smelled mysterious. He kept his door closed. He had secrets. His new girlfriend, Linda, would sometimes appear in moccasins and ripped jeans, and the two of them carried a frightening air of sexuality about them.

For sixteen hundred dollars, Skip bought a lime-green VW Bug with his earnings from his summer job at a discount store called Zayre. He was working there again this year, and that was where he was when the boy in the white Bug pulled up in front of our house.

At thirteen, I was bored and weepy, trapped at home in a neighborhood next to exactly nothing. Some Saturdays I walked the mile to the new shopping mall, where the movie theater played foreign and R-rated films. Looking back now, I realize how odd it was for a mall in Warwick, Rhode Island, to have such a thing. But it was part of my peculiar landscape that summer. I would walk to the mall, spend hours in the record shop and bookstore, then watch *Women in Love*. A restaurant across from the movie theater had baskets of peanuts on every table and the idea was to eat the peanuts and throw the shells on the floor, a decadent pleasure that I loved. There was also a Newport Creamery, a local restaurant chain, on the second floor where college girls wore green-and-white-striped uniforms and scooped ice cream with a truculence that I envied.

On that long walk to and from the mall, I worried over the sad state of my life: too young to date or drive, yet keenly aware of something bigger out there waiting for me. My yearning for this something was enough to keep me up at night or send me into fits of agony and sobs. I would sit in my room and play the forty-five of "Candles in the Rain" by Melanie as loud as I could, until my father would shout up the stairs: "Put me and that woman out of our misery, please!" At which point I would switch from Melanie to Simon and Garfunkel's album *Parsley, Sage, Rosemary and Thyme* and cry over "The Dangling Conversation." When they sang: "And you read your Emily Dickinson, and I my Robert Frost...," my entire being ached for a boy who read poetry, a boy who would love me.

I spent many late afternoons perched at the top of the stairs, gazing out the window. We—my parents, my brother and I—lived with my grandmother, Mama Rose, in the house she had moved into when she was two years old. She'd given birth to ten children in the bedroom where she still slept, and six of those children still lived within walking distance. From that window, I could see the rooftops of three of their houses. I used to play a game. *Someday I will go beyond those houses, beyond the mall, beyond those distant trees. Someday I will go farther than anything I can see at this moment....*

This was what I was doing when outside the window I watched a white VW Bug turn the corner onto our street and park behind my parents' green Chevy Caprice. The door opened. Out stepped a boy with long pale blond hair, as skinny as can be, dressed in that summer's uniform of torn jeans and pocket T-shirt. He disappeared up the front walk that led to our kitchen door. I held my breath. Then a deep voice asked, "Skip home yet?" Next came my parents' muffled voices, the creaky sound of the screen door opening and then swinging shut, and the boy was in our house. I ran to my room and brushed my waist-length blond hair, sniffed under my arms for any traces of BO, then walked downstairs, trying to look cool and casual.

When I entered the kitchen, where they all sat, the boy and my father holding bottles of Michelob, he stood up the way gentlemen in movies do. My heart was doing strange and wonderful things: flutters and leaps and banging about. He said his name, which was so beautifully ordinary I almost wept at the sound of it. He sat back down. I sat across from him at our table with the tablecloth decorated with tulips and topped with plastic stretching between us.

"This is Skip's sister, Ann," my father said.

My father went on to ask him about studying chemistry in college and his own summer job at a nearby lab and the entire time the boy snuck blue-eyed glances at me and gave me closemouthed smiles. Too soon, my brother came home from work and the two of them left in the white Bug. I raced upstairs and watched them go, the eggbeater sound of that engine growing faint in the summer night as they disappeared from my sight.

Skip worked at Zayre until nine o'clock most nights. But the boy came for him at eight, or even earlier, and sat at our kitchen table across from me, drinking a beer with my father and eating my grandmother's meatball sandwiches.

"What does that boy think?" Mama Rose said one night a week or so into this ritual. "We dumb or something? He come here to see Ann, not Skip."

My father's own blue eyes bulged. "She's *thirteen,* for Christ's sake," he said. "I'll fucking kill him."

But I knew in my heart it was true. This college boy liked me. *Me!* Over those nights, I'd learned that his father had just died, a fact that made my crush on him grow even bigger. Here was a boy who knew tragedy and poetry, who knew history and philosophy. It was as if he had stepped out of my imagination and into my kitchen. Suddenly, my dull life had become thrilling. After my brother would come home and the two of them would leave, I could barely sit still. I hopped and danced and talked fast. I went outside to stare at the moon. I begged my mother to take me for a drive, which she sometimes did. We'd go to the Dunkin' Donuts and sit in the pink seats and she'd tell me her own teenaged love stories.

One night, on his way out the door, the boy paused. He handed me a worn paperback—*Siddhartha* by Hermann Hesse.

"I thought you might like this," he said with his bashful smile. I took it, still warm from his pocket, and nodded like an idiot.

"So," he said, making sure my parents were out of earshot, "do you want to go to the movies tomorrow night?"

My ears started to ring so loudly I wasn't sure I'd heard him right. "Sure," I managed through my dry mouth.

Then he was gone, down the sidewalk where my brother waited for him.

It didn't occur me to even ask my parents if I could go to the movies with him. I was young enough that I'd never done anything yet that required permission. I basically went nowhere, except the mall, and did nothing without them. So when he showed up earlier than usual the next night, I simply came down the stairs and said, "We're going to the movies." Mama Rose jumped up and my father looked bewildered, but I just walked out the door and into that white Bug.

It smelled so masculine in there, I thought I might faint. Smoky and musky and leathery. I inhaled deeply and clutched the edge of my seat and concentrated on the way the veins in his hand looked as he shifted. The movie was *Claire's Knee*, a French film at the mall. I tried to follow it, to read the subtitles as they appeared across the screen, but there was too much going on in my head and my heart. I wished someone was there to see me at a French film with a college boy. But none of my friends would ever be here now.

The movie was about a guy trying to touch Claire's knee. At least, that was all I could manage to take from it. Mostly the movie for me was about the few times the boy's arm brushed against mine when he shifted in his seat and the smell of his own particular scent.

"Have you ever had the strawberry pie at Cello's?" he asked me when we got back in the car.

I shook my head. I'd never even heard of Cello's. But soon enough we were there and he was ordering two pieces of strawberry pie and two coffees. The pie was delicious, a huge mound of sweetened whole strawberries topped with whipped cream. I'd stayed up the entire night before reading *Siddhartha,* and we ate pie and talked about the book and about Hermann Hesse, Simon and Garfunkel's lyrics running through my mind the whole time.

Sitting in front of my house a couple of hours later, he told me that he'd had a girlfriend named Kathy for a couple of years. She worked at the Newport Creamery. "But it's kind of on and off," he said sadly.

I nodded, trying to seem sympathetic and wise.

"So that's okay?" he asked.

"Uh, sure," I said, confused.

He smiled at me. "Good," he said. "How about we go to the beach tomorrow?"

I nodded again.

He handed me a copy of *The Tin Drum* by Günter Grass and I somehow managed to open the car door and walk up the sidewalk and into my house.

The next day he picked me up at ten o'clock in the morning. My parents were at work, but it still hadn't occurred to me that they might not allow me to go with him. We drove to a beach I had never been to before. It was called East Beach, and something in the way the beach faced the ocean made the waves there enormous and rough. We bodysurfed, getting tumbled and thrown onto the sand until we could hardly walk back to the scratchy army blanket he'd brought. Panting, I dropped onto it beside him, trying not to stare at the V of hair that started on his chest and trailed down to his belly and into his trunks.

He produced two warm cans of beer from his rucksack. I watched him pop the tops on both and then hand one to me.

"So where are you going to school in the fall?" he asked me.

I frowned. "The same place," I said.

"Really?" he said. "For some reason I thought next year was your first year."

I thought I understood then. "No, I'm not in high school yet. I'm going into ninth grade."

The boy put his beer down. "What?" But before I could repeat what I'd said, he said, "You're not going to college in September?"

I laughed. "College? I'm only thirteen."

"Oh my God," he said. "No wonder Skip said he was going to beat the shit out of me."

The boy in the white VW Bug did not walk out of my life that day. He simply stopped trying to date me. Instead, he introduced me to the world that was waiting for me to grow up and enter. He taught me to play Frisbee. He took me to see the play *Hair*. He drove me an hour to Cambridge and we went to see experimental theater, to shop at Marimekko, to eat vegetarian food. Some afternoons he took me into Providence, a fifteen-minute drive from my own small town but a city with art stores and restaurants and theaters. He introduced me to a guy who made and sold fringed vests, and I had him make me a purple one with beads in the fringes. He bought hamburgers stuffed into pita bread and ice cream with M&M's folded into it. We browsed the College Hill Bookstore together, and he bought me copies of poetry by Gregory Corso and Lawrence Ferlinghetti. He played FM radio in his car. He explained physics and existentialism to me.

For three summers, he drove up in his white Bug when he came home from college, and led me through the complicated and confusing world of adolescence.

And then came the summer that I was sixteen, and over the school year had acquired a boyfriend. I was sitting in the backyard, waiting for that boyfriend to pick me up, when I heard the familiar eggbeater sound of a VW engine. The boy walked toward me, grinning.

"Want to go to Boston?" he asked. "There's a new show at the MFA."

For the first time since I'd known him, I said, "No. I have a date."

What was that look that came over his face? Disappointment? Surprise? Maybe even hurt?

He studied me, sixteen at last, and he nodded and said, "Okay."

As I watched him walk away, I realized my crush on him had ended, replaced now with a more mature affection and passion for the boy who would be appearing in a few minutes.

One might think the story would end there. But it didn't. It hasn't ended yet.

The boy in the white Bug continues to appear on my doorstep. He got married and had children and moved to Washington, D.C. But every now and then, my doorbell rings and he is standing there. "Want to grab a coffee?" he might ask. And I go off with him in his Volvo station wagon to talk about books and life.

A month ago, on a winter Sunday morning, my doorbell rang and there he was. His mother had died recently and he was home to clean out her house and sell it. I made coffee and we sat together, reminiscing about her and her little Yorkie, Dolittle.

"Guess what I found?" he said. "The bill of sale for my old white Bug."

Tears came to my eyes. I could picture him in that car, with his long pale blond hair, teaching me about the world. I could still smell that masculine smell, smoke and musk and leather. If I closed my eyes, he was that boy again, and I was that girl with the crush on him that I thought would never end.

He held out a fabric case. "For you," he said.

I opened it to find knitting needles of every size inside.

"I brought my mother's yarn and needles to her church knitting group," he explained. "They took the yarn, but they said the needles should go to someone special."

I pressed the case against me, still warm from where it had rested in his jacket. Even though it was winter, in that moment I could taste strawberries and ocean air. We've never talked about what we each felt back in that summer of 1970, or any of the summers that followed. Perhaps we don't need to. For some things, I know now, words are not sufficient.

# Creative Writing

## David Levithan

There's no real story here—but isn't that true for most crushes? Or maybe there is a story, but it's just not the one I thought I was living at the time. That's true for most crushes, too.

I was a freshman in college, and I got into a creative writing class. It would end up being the only creative writing class I would ever take, but that's immaterial. It was my second semester, and I was proud I'd made the cut. Almost everyone else in the class was older than me. Including Jamie Walker.

Jamie Walker was from the town I lived in the first year of my life, only two towns over from the town where I lived for the rest of my life (up until college). He had dark curly hair, was about my height. I can't remember the color of his eyes, but I do remember they had a glimmer to them, the glimmer that people who are engaged by life tend to have. I am much more of a sucker for cute than hot, and he was definitely cute. Or at least in my memory he is. I could easily take my face book down from my bookshelf (that's small *f* face book—it's a real book) and check. But I'm so much older than him now, and that two-year difference made him so much older than me then. I don't want to alter that imbalance. I want to remember him as he was, even if that memory's vague, and perhaps even wrong. Who he was to me matters so much more than who he actually was.

This was 1991; it's important to note that. This was before email, before *Ellen*, before you could turn on your computer and see the world. This was before I knew I was gay, before I knew that kissing boys wasn't just something that happened, but was something I wanted to do. This was before I felt I could call myself a writer, before I had really written anything truly good.

Our class met in the library, which would have been romantic if it hadn't been one of those modern libraries where all you feel is the concrete, not the books. Our professor was an MFA student who later went on to publish nothing whatsoever that I can find. Her teaching methodology seemed to be "If you can't say something nice, say nothing at all." Which left her largely silent as we tore each other apart.

In the absence of an instructor's heavy hand, a creative writing seminar becomes a cauldron of hurt feelings, cutthroat ambition, unbridled defensiveness, and tenuous alliances that would make any third-rate parliament proud. From the very first day, you try to find your allies, and then, as the critiques come in, you reassess your allegiances. I don't remember a lot about the other people who were in our class—there was a science fiction writer who confounded us with his syntax and the way the letter *z* could crop up in each and every one of his characters' names. And then there was the girl who'd written a piece about a bad breakup and then burst into tears when I pointed out the main character wasn't very likable. (I learned a very valuable lesson then: treat all breakup stories as autobiography, just in case.) And there was one guy who spent at least five minutes harping on the fact that the character in one of my stories had tried to spot a Volkswagen as he drove a long road in Michigan. "Why a Volkswagen?" he kept asking. I tried to tell him there was no deeper meaning to it, but he didn't believe me.

I can't remember what that guy looked like, but I can remember that as the weather got warmer and spring came, Jamie Walker wore V-neck T-shirts. I don't think I'd ever seen anyone wear an undershirt as a shirt before, especially a V-neck. If I hadn't already had a crush on him, the V-neck would have sent me spiraling—I, who never looked at necks, would find myself studying his neck. I, who was never distracted by the space below the neck, was suddenly drawn there. My own chest was already hairy—a fact I had no desire to share with the world. But there were some stray hairs in the deeper part of his V, an echo of the occasional stubble on his chin. What I felt was desire, but it was a confused desire. Did I want to touch that space, trace that trail, or did I simply want to be that body myself? Did I find him attractive, or did I wish to be that attractive? It was the openness that was sexy, and it was the openness that I lacked.

We liked each other's writing. That was clear early on. When all the critiques of my pages would be passed back to me, his handwriting was the one I sought out. We sat next to or near each other and often would talk on the way out of class. But we'd always go our separate ways once we reached the bottom of the library steps.

I might have forgotten about him. (A catalog of crushes is an oft-revised thing, and sometimes older crushes get lost in the revision.) But our professor surprised us one day with an assignment—we were to swap stories with another person in class and deconstruct one another's writing. Poems could be turned into stories; stories could be turned into poems. We could choose our partners. And Jamie chose me.

The next week we swapped stories. Not just on paper but electronically—which meant, at the time, on a disk. I waited until I was back in my room to read his. I was alone—I can remember this. My roommate was gone. I was nervous and excited—the two most applicable adjectives for a crush. I had given Jamie a story about a family where the grandfather is a tyrant and the grandson, tired of trying to live up to him, accidentally shoots him in a hunting accident. I was proud of this story, even if it was, as most of my fiction was, entirely fictional, without many details of my own life scattered around. Jamie's stories, from what I can recall, were usually about college students doing foolish things—either in friendship or in romance. I expected more of the same but loved the fact that he had written it knowing that I would be its first reader.

His story started plainly enough, with two high school boys watching *L.A. Law*. For those of you not watching 10:00 p.m. shows in 1991, *L.A. Law* was about...well, a group of lawyers in L.A. They were vain, troubled, comic, and usually won their cases. The men were sexy in that corny 1980s way—hair a-poof, muscles worked out, abs yet an indicator for beauty. Not my type. I was holding out for River Phoenix. Or, if I had to settle, Keanu Reeves.

In the story, there's a tension between the boys as they watch *L.A. Law*—romantic tension. Relationship tension. And then the scene shifts, and you're in the *L.A. Law* episode. Two of the male characters are arguing. But there's also romantic, relationship tension between them. And then, right when you think it's going to erupt into a fight, they start making out. Jimmy Smits and Corbin Bernsen. Or maybe Jimmy Smits and Blair Underwood. I can't remember which. But suddenly, the clothes were coming off. The need was overpowering. Belts were undone; pants were shed. And the kisses were real. These were two men who were in love with each other, and their kisses were real.

I had read hundreds of books up to that point. I had read hundreds of stories. I had copies of Jackie Collins and Nancy Friday and Ken Follett that opened up on their own to the sex scenes, because I had consulted them so often. But nothing I had read had prepared me for this. I had never known that reading words on a page could give you the same sensation as someone breathing on your neck, running his hand over your arm, undoing the top button of your pants. I had never known that a story could convey the feeling of a hard kiss, a warm body, fingers under elastic. I had known words could capture the mechanics, but not the intensity. But here were these characters—grasping, longing, battling, letting go. I believed them. And, somewhere unacknowledged but getting louder, I knew I wanted to be them. I wanted to be like that. And I wanted to write like that.

I was going to fail the assignment, because I didn't want to change a thing. Sure, a word or two, here or there. I was fine editing it. But I couldn't deconstruct it. I couldn't rearrange it, alter it, make it into something else. I tried. I tried playing it backward. I tried inverting the frame. I tried everything short of making them characters from *Hill Street Blues* instead of *L.A. Law*. But ultimately I couldn't change it. It had to be what it was.

Jamie, if you're out there, why did you give me this story? Did you know what I was, and know that I didn't really know it yet? Was it a flirtation, or even something more than that? Or did it just happen to be the story that was on your computer on the day the assignment was given? Did you just happen to turn on *L.A. Law* that night and decide to play with it a little, not really giving any thought as to who its first reader would be? Did you mean to tell me something, or did you just tell me something, anyway?

Nervous and excited, nervous and excited. I was nervous about that next class but couldn't tell anyone about it. I was excited about that next class but couldn't tell anyone about it.

In the story I want to tell, I wrote a little note at the bottom of what he wrote. When he saw it, he smiled and told me we should talk about it after class. For an hour we sat there as girls read their blood poetry and the science fiction boy told us about the time Zaffir and Zazzlow traversed the space-time continuum in order to fetch the dread mineral Zylon out of the grasp of the cruel overlord Zartra. Our expectation bloomed into something more certain than expectation, and our nervousness solidified into something closer to intent. When the class ended, we wordlessly led each other to the back of the library, to a carrel far from any other student, and that was where he kissed me, that was where I finally got to touch that neck, that chest, that was where my hand pressed against that V-neck and his hand lowered down my back. That was where I cried because I had gotten what I wanted. That was when the joy of it was so much that I actually cried, because finally I had found what I was looking for, and it wasn't just him. It was everything. When he saw I was crying, his kisses changed into something more comforting, something that understood. And he whispered, "Shh shh," and then made a joke that made it all okay, that made me kiss him again, that made me lead him back out, holding his hand, to go get some dinner, to go walk through the night, to stay up with each other, then sleep with each other, to greet the next morning as if it was ours together.

But I didn't write a note at the bottom of what he wrote—at least, not that note. I don't even know if I told him how much I liked it; I might have just said how hard it was to cut down. He had taken my short story and turned it from fifteen pages to something like three, jutting phrases against each other to create a prose poem of indeterminate meaning. I think later on he told me he'd liked some of my edits on his story, but that was it.

I never ended up seeing him out of class. Not in person. Toward the end of the year, the newspaper I was working at ran a two-page spread of photos from our university's Gay, Lesbian and Bisexual Ball. There were a few photos of him there, dressed—if I am remembering correctly—in a sleeveless number that would have made Audrey Hepburn proud. I was no doubt hanging out with my dorm friends that night, swathed in flannel, watching *Twin Peaks*, enjoying myself in a different way.

I never took another writing class. But gay characters started appearing in my fiction. Sometimes they knew they were gay. Sometimes they didn't. Sometimes I knew they were gay. Sometimes I didn't. Not until later. I could revise the stories, but I couldn't revise the fact of my previous obliviousness. I don't want to.

I don't write this with any regret. My life unfolded the way that it did, and that led to the life I have now, for which I am grateful. The difference between a crush and a love is its viability. I could try to revise the past into a world where Jamie and I could have been together. But that wasn't the world my head was living in at the time.

It is often the case that at the end of the crush, the only thing you've learned is how to better deal with a crush the next time one comes along. In this case, I got a little more. Whether or not he meant to—and I strongly suspect he didn't—Jamie Walker made me a better writer. Or at least he opened up something in that part of me. The rest, in time, would follow.

# Three Little Words

## Lauren Oliver

As a teenager, I hated the word *crush*. It reminded me of a word my mother would use and so (predictably) it annoyed me. It reminded me of being babied and condescended to and patted on the head, or reminded me to eat vegetables and stop slouching.

The fact of the matter is, when I was in high school, I did not have crushes on people. I fell in *love*.

I fell in love with (in order): Mike Netto, Rob Massa, Kent McWilliams, Willem DeVries, Matty Campbell, Matthew Furey, John Fink, some guy at Starbucks whose name I no longer remember and who wore (I'm ashamed to say) enormous spacers in his ears, Jeremy Tucker, Rob Massa again, the bartender at Peabody's, Rob Massa *again*.

Never mind that I never even *spoke* to some (okay, fine—all) of these people. That wasn't the point. I lived in a small, affluent town that abided strictly by all the most tired clichés. Houses were beautiful and clean. Everyone studied hard and played sports and applied to schools like Harvard, Yale and Duke. Lawns were mowed religiously and people talked about the stock market and new car models.

And nothing ever happened.

We were, quite simply, bored out of our freaking minds. We needed a reason to get up and go to school in the morning—and European history, Advanced Placement, wouldn't cut it. We needed a reason to spend hours getting ready on Friday nights, just to attend basement parties with the exact same group of people we saw daily in the hallways. We needed to believe in change—that today, tonight, this instant, with a single word or look or perfect pair of black stretch pants, our lives might suddenly and radically open up in front of us, the whole vista of ordinary suburban life dropping away to reveal some glittering, sumptuous, romantic paradise underneath.

In other words, we needed hope. It was, in some ways, an extension of the kind of childhood thinking that seeks to apprehend the whole world in terms of magic, in terms of the fantastic and unbelievable things that might conceal themselves in ordinary places: fairies in flower petals, princes in frog (or emo drama-boy) form.

But maybe the point *was* that I didn't speak to any of the people I "loved" throughout the years: whole romantic affairs could be and were an invention, a big adolescent game of make-believe. I could imagine that beneath the sullen scowl of a grunting football player lay the soul of a poet. I could pretend that the senior who gave me a momentary flickering glance in the cafeteria was really trying to communicate the depth of his feelings for me. The love was not unrequited—no. It *couldn't* be, precisely because it remained unspoken.

And in my head, everyone always loved me back.

So I never *really* had my heart broken, even though I cried for hours when Rob Massa started dating Beth Jonap, and ate ice cream for a week when Mike Netto kissed Annie Rana by the cafeteria. I was *crushed;* I got the air whooshed out of me like a punch to the gut, had a feeling like a rock in my stomach plenty of times. But I wasn't heartbroken, not really.

Heartbreak had to wait until I fell in love for real, and falling in love for real had to wait until Steve Gaynor.

Steve and I began dating just after I graduated from high school. I was working as a lifeguard at a local swim and tennis club; he worked behind the snack bar. From the beginning, our relationship had all the makings of an epic romance. It was summertime. Our relationship was discouraged by our parents (my parents thought I could do better than him; his thought he could do better than me) *and* it was something of a secret, because I had briefly dated his best friend, Dan, the summer before, who also worked at the pool club.

The year before, in fact, I remember I had been undecided about which best friend was the most crush worthy. Dan was polite, blond, a Catholic; Steve was Italian, dark-haired, endlessly sarcastic, and extremely dismissive of my tentative attempts to charm him with my wit (and bikini collection). I liked them both in a vague and undifferentiated way, as years of falling "in love" with boys from the other side of the cafeteria and classroom had taught me to do; in other words, I liked them with little to no knowledge of or regard for their personalities. When it comes to love, teenagers are a little bit like black holes: they will eagerly and hungrily slurp up anything that comes within their orbit. At least, that's what I was like. I was a black hole for affection, attention, for anything that could even pass as love. When Dan asked me to the movies, I said yes, and so I dated Dan first.

Of course, Dan and I had very little in common and, as a result, next to nothing to talk about, which proved problematic when he returned to Villanova in the fall and our conversations were limited primarily to phone contact. After Dan and I broke up, Steve and I stayed in touch (ahh, the wonders of the internet); he was every bit as sarcastic, and every bit as immune to my attempts to charm him as he had ever been, which of course made him infuriating—and absolutely worth pursuing.

Steve and I chatted over IM; then we began to talk on the phone. (Steve was in his sophomore year of college in Massachusetts. High school graduation was approaching for me, and with it, the last halcyon summer of lifeguarding and living at home and drinking with friends in backyards and in basements and feeling as though time would stretch always, and endlessly, around us, keeping us forever golden and tan and young and happy.) I had done many, many things with boys—I had even had sex by then (sorry, Mom)—but I had never before actually talked to a boy.

Obviously I had *spoken* to boys. I'd had an official boyfriend, after all (a fact I had paraded just as proudly and ostentatiously as a jockey leading a Preakness winner around the track). But I had never *really* talked to a boy, the way I talked to my very best friends. *Cosmo* and *Seventeen*—and all the other magazines I devoured at the time—had prepared me to flirt and trick and swagger, to fake confidence and "hook" a guy by means as varied (and suspicious) as the selection of my lip gloss to the adoption of new hobbies and interests ("Show him you can hang with the boys: read up on his favorite sport!"). But they had not taught me to connect—to share, to be shared with.

In the months leading up to the summer we were to spend together, Steve and I spent countless hours on the phone. We talked. And talked. And talked. We talked about art, and science, and God, and drugs; about frat parties, and house parties, and parents, and siblings; about what we wanted in life, and what we were afraid of, and what we disliked about ourselves (and even about each other). On the afternoon preceding spring homecoming, I got home from school and called Steve. Seven hours and twenty-two ignored call-waiting interruptions later, I was *still* on the phone with Steve, happy as I'd ever been, even though the dance was winding down, my pretty new dress was hanging in my closet, tags on, and my friends were absolutely furious with me.

A funny thing happened over the course of those months: while Steve and I talked and the rest of the world did something, presumably, I fell in love with Steve. Not a Steve of my imagining and not a Steve of my invention, not a Steve who *would be if he would just notice me* or *could be if he would only so-and-so* or *break up with what's-her-name,* or *look my way* or *change a bit* or *notice me* or *blah blah blah.*

I fell in love with Steve Gaynor, whose voice was low and warm and reassuring, even when he was arguing with me; who could not only have made arguing with me a competitive sport, but been its Lance Armstrong or Tiger Woods; who could, apart from infuriating me consistently, always diffuse my anger with a laugh, and distract me with a story, and surprise me with his sensitivity. As I said, I fell in love for real.

He, miraculously, was falling in love with me right back—with *me* me, not the *Cosmo*-inspired, lip-gloss me or some other *me* of his own invention, but with *me* as I understood myself, a girl who was silly and smart and ferocious and defensive and needy and hurt and desperate to love and desperate to be loved back. And in doing so, he performed the oldest and most powerful magic of all, the kind of stuff that moves worlds and rearranges, forever, the path and trajectory of lives, a magic as vast and powerful as any of the forces that shape the known universe: he reached into my own personal universe, into the constellation of me, and found a way to close the black hole.

Nothing had prepared me for the feeling of loving somebody who would actually—not fictionally—love me back, and tell me so. A crush is to love as a forty-watt bulb is to a fireworks display: the principle of illumination is the same, but the scope places them in entirely different categories.

The first time Steve and I kissed, he had been home from college for less than a week. He drove to my house in the middle of a downpour. The sky was purple and the rain came down in sheets, like whole descending walls of metal. After months of talking on the phone, sharing intimate stories and details about our lives, we were both nervous and shy at first. I remember vividly what I was wearing: a tight white tank top, under which my 34Bs were desperately attempting to impress in their push-up bra, and cutoff shorts so tiny they could have easily doubled for underwear. (The outfit was inspired, no doubt, from other lessons I had taken to heart after years of absorbing "women's" magazines—*Show some skin! Guys love legs! Can you be casual and sexy? Yes!*)

We sat on the couch together, and for once our conversation did not come easily. The noise of the rain was tremendous. I had just gotten my second tattoo: a large ouroboros on my lower back. The ouroboros is a snake or a dragon consuming its own tail, an ancient symbol of regeneration or rebirth. Steve asked to see it. I hitched my shirt to my waist, feeling unaccountably nervous, swiveling away from him, and in that moment I was truly aware for the first time of how many inches and centimeters of my skin were exposed; it seemed like every last one of them came alive at that second, all the spaces of my body lighting up at once. He traced his finger carefully around my tattoo, and it felt like fire everywhere he touched. Possibly, you know, because I'd *just* gotten the tattoo and no one was supposed to touch it—but even when his hands moved to my waist, to turn me around, the fire was still there, like comets blazing a trail under his fingers.

And when we kissed, I swear there were fireworks.

I had been trying to make my small town more interesting by pretending that certain people in it were special; but once I found someone who thought that *I* was special, my small town exploded, expanded, became fascinating and gorgeous and mysterious. We had sex in the backseat of his Jeep (again—sorry, Mom) while outside the woods whispered and swayed, impossible, enormous curtains of green moving in rhythm. Parking lots shimmered and glittered in the heat; air conditioners sang out Steve's name; beer tasted like his lips, like kissing him; sweat was his body and my body and our bodies; the very air reformed itself forever into those three magical words: *I love you.*

At work, however, Steve insisted that we pretend to be just friends. He was afraid that if Dan found out...what? There would be a fistfight? Dan would suddenly recover passionate feelings for me he had obviously never had in the first place? It was never totally clear to me, but I didn't object too strongly. It made the whole thing sordid and exciting, like having an affair without having to bother with the whole marriage and infidelity thing. We communicated through shared looks, stealing occasional, fleeting touches when no one was looking.

At night, the staff would sneak into the pool club to host parties; before leaving for the day, we would crank up the heat in the pool so it would be warm for us later. When we returned around ten or eleven, steam would rise in wisps and curls from the surface of the water. We would open up the snack bar and eat ice cream and frozen Snickers bars with our warm Coors Light and rum. When everyone was sufficiently tipsy, we would all make a run for the pool, shrieking and laughing, scattering clothes as we went, and diving and flipping and pushing each other into the water.

While everyone drank and swam and attempted to make grilled cheese and crushed Dorito sandwiches (drunkenness is, after all, the mother of culinary invention), Steve and I snuck up to the old, disused shuffleboard courts, which were surrounded on all sides by ancient trees, and cold even during the day. The courts were covered by a thick layering of pine needles, which muffled our footsteps as we walked, and the moon shone down frostily through the black arms of the trees. We stood there, shivering and kissing. (At least, I shivered. Steve seemed to be half reptile; he hardly ever got cold.)

During the day, it was agony to be so close to Steve and be unable to touch him and kiss him, but it was agony of the delicious kind: we shared a secret, which extended between us, tethering us together, like an invisible cord. When I think about that summer—and our romance in general—I think of that curious admixture of intense pleasure and sharp pain, like the ache in your limbs and chest after you've just sprinted a very long way: a winding down, a happiness in being through, a joy in having pushed yourself to the end of something; and also some regret for all the distance you've covered so quickly, a distance you can never get back. Even when I was with Steve, it seems to me I was already nostalgic for our love and already mourning its end.

Because our relationship had a final magical element, it was doomed to failure from the start. In the fall, I was starting my freshman year at the University of Chicago. Steve was returning to Massachusetts. Of course, this made our promises to love each other forever more, not less, fervent.

And then, of course, it ended.

Let me tell you something: when you *imagine* someone might be in love with you, and then you can no longer imagine that they might secretly be in love with you due to insurmountable factual evidence (a new girlfriend, graduation, the outing of a sexual preference that precludes you from the running), it hurts. That is, as everyone always points out, why they call it a crush and not a *lift* or a *bounce*.

But when you *know* someone is in love with you, and then one day that person *stops* being in love with you—that, my friends, is total annihilation. That is heartbreak.

Love, unlike diamond jewelry and despite what inspirational embroidered pillows might tell you, does not necessarily last forever, and learning this for the first time was deeply traumatic. After Steve dumped me, I spent my first week and a half of college in a near daze. I wandered around campus and refused to remove my sunglasses, even at night, in order to conceal my enormously puffy eyes, a result of near-continuous crying. (I then had to spend the remainder of my four years at the University of Chicago trying to prove, with differing degrees of success, that I wasn't entirely unstable—or, alternatively, some crazy Corey Hart–eighties music fan who believed that aviators should be a midnight fashion statement.)

Interestingly, I found that in order to get over my heartbreak, I required—in addition to gallons of Ben & Jerry's Chocolate Fudge

Brownie Ice Cream—a different kind of junk food: silly, fluffy, from-afar, pipe-dream crushes. I needed to crush on guys who might not talk to me, sure, but would certainly not dump me *over IM* (ahhh, the wonders of the internet) after bonding with some sorority girl named Becky at a frat party. (Hmmm. Maybe I'm not *entirely* over it.)

The point is, the word *crush* stopped bothering me. Crushes are like Snickers bars for the heart. Sure, they won't sustain you forever—everyone needs more solid sustenance—but they make long afternoons *way* more tolerable.

Love is transformative. It changes you. As a result, it changes the world for you. It is worth pursuing and fighting for; it is worth intercontinental flights and tearful phone conversations and broken-plate fights; it is even worth the crippling pain of its occasional dissolution. It gives us meaning and magic. It makes life seem better and deeper than, well, life.

And in the meantime, I'm happy to settle for my newest crush: the barista at DUB Pies in Brooklyn. You should see the way he makes an Australian flat white, all dark, chocolate-scented coffee and a pretty kidney-bean-shaped dribble of espresso piped into the thick, creamy topping of foamed milk. He says that the kidney-bean-shaped symbol is just that: a kidney bean.

But I'm pretty sure it's a heart.

That, my friends, is love. Or close enough.

# How Duran Duran Saved My Life

## Katherine Center

Funny story. Back in 1984, when I was twelve and Duran Duran was on a world tour, they happened to come to my hometown of Houston. And they happened to stay not far from my neighborhood. And one afternoon, on their way back to the hotel, their stretch limo happened to get a flat tire. Right out in front of my house.

They needed to use a phone to call a mechanic. So they got out of the car, walked up the nearest sidewalk and rang my bell.

You can imagine how fortunate that was for me, since I happened to be home that day. In fact, I was not only home, but dancing in our family room at that very moment to a VHS collection of their videos. Not dancing too hard, of course—just enough to give my face a little flush and brighten up my eyes.

My two best friends were there, too. And when we heard the doorbell, we thought it was probably a pesky neighbor. We almost ignored it. But then it rang again. And something about the sound of it had a kind of urgency that caught my attention. I decided to answer. Lucky for me, I was wearing my best jeans. And I had the good sense to pause on the way to the door and apply some lip gloss.

Because the sight that greeted me on our front porch left me breathless: all five members of Duran Duran, as tall as I'd always imagined they'd be and decked out in leather coats and rocker gear, were smiling at me and introducing themselves like they weren't even famous at all.

I showed remarkable poise as I shook all their hands and invited them in. And before I knew it, we'd made ourselves comfortable on my mother's living room furniture as they told me all about their world tour. We shot the breeze as we waited for a mechanic to arrive, and it did not take long before I started to notice their eyes lingering, more than anywhere else, on me.

A note, here, about the twelve-year-old me: I was—to say it kindly—awkward. But that didn't seem to matter. Because by the end of the afternoon, quite without my knowledge, those five sensitive rockers had glimpsed my inner beauty and fallen desperately, passionately, almost life-threateningly in love with me.

Which happens a lot.

It's probably clear by now that this story is not exactly true. It didn't really happen. In truth, I'm telling the story of a story—one I wrote on paper with little gnomes in the corners over twenty-five years ago.

But what's amazing to me, as I pull that fictional story from my memory, is that it's shelved right alongside things that were real. And now, all these years later, faded by time, that story feels not unlike my memories of actual moments from true life. I can see the shy way John Taylor ducked his head as he apologized for interrupting my day. I can see Simon Le Bon's long fingers drumming nervously on the striped upholstery of my mother's fanciest chair.

Eventually in the story, Simon would wind up proposing to me—though only after I'd rejected and broken the hearts of every other band member. And I would make him the happiest man in the world by saying yes. And as much as I fully understand that I never did actually marry—or even meet, or even see in person—Simon Le Bon, when I go to YouTube now and watch those videos from my childhood, I feel all kinds of tenderness. It comes back to me in 3-D. I watched certain videos of theirs a thousand times at least. I memorized lyrics and dance steps and facial expressions. And now when I see that face of Simon's, which I swooned over so relentlessly for so long, I find myself wanting to give a little sigh of nostalgia over all the good times we shared.

A quick snapshot of me in sixth grade: Buckteeth and braces. Lots of freckles. National Science Olympiad finalist (one of six, and the only girl). School uniform. Sneakers. Desperately crushed out on a boy in my class who was entirely and permanently out of my league.

I had two best friends in sixth grade, and we were all equally miserable. We wanted to be beautiful, but we knew we weren't. We wanted to have social power, but we knew we didn't. We wanted not to feel horrible about ourselves, but we didn't seem to have a choice.

And so we suffered through the school week, agonizing over clothing choices and who sat near who at the lunch table. We made lists of areas for self-improvement and drew diagrams of the social landscape. We made fun of ourselves, too. We might have been hopeless dorks, but, at the very least, unlike the lowest of the low, we knew we were dorks. We had the good sense to scorn ourselves properly.

That's something that really strikes me about that time in my life. How crucially important it seemed to let everyone know that I didn't like me, either. I spent that year, and one or two that followed, trying to get as far away from myself as possible. It was the beginning of a profound split—this feeling that *my body wasn't me*.

It was my first experience with an aspect of womanhood that's so normal I hardly even notice it anymore: the way that, when you are walking down a street as a woman, you are both the woman walking and, at the same time, an anonymous audience watching the woman walking. You do a thing and watch yourself doing it at the same time. You live inside your body and outside of it at the same time. You are both observer and observed.

And being watched like that changes your life. You know you're being judged. You know it because you can hear yourself thinking—and it's you who is doing the judging. And so you check your reflection in mirrors, or get a perm, or start refusing to leave the house without lipstick on. Just to pass your own muster.

Safe to say, in sixth grade, I could not pass anybody's muster. Least of all mine.

So that was where I lived back then—in that hollow place between who I wanted to be and who I actually was.

Except on the weekends.

On the weekends, I felt better. My two best friends and I had sleepovers. We ate pizza and watched *Friday Night Videos*, and then we'd curl up in each other's beds, pull out our novels and read them out loud to each other. And no matter how mean we were to ourselves all week long, on Friday nights, we got to take a break. Because if the guys from Duran Duran were as in love with us as they were, we couldn't be all bad. Right?

And they were in love. Desperately in love. Poor Simon wept over and over again when he thought he couldn't have me. Nick punched a wall with his fist, John stormed out of rooms, and both Roger and Andy became paralyzed with longing and had to take to their beds.

Oh, we had some adventures. We moved to New York City, we took a vacation to a mountain cabin, we fought, we kissed, we accepted and rejected various engagement rings, and we quote-unquote *had sex* (though I didn't actually know what it was, I knew it was very important and something you did only with people who had taken hold of your very soul). But every adventure was a result of—or a setup for, or a diversion from—love.

It was a lot of pressure on me as the main character. After all, there were five of them and only one of me. I had to choose between five gorgeous men who might literally perish if they couldn't have me. I had to ruin at least four lives.

In real life, I was lucky if a boy even talked to me. In real life, I did not want to be looked at or even seen. In real life, I was all wrong. So I just tried not to think about real life.

Of course, at the time, my problems seemed very unique. I believed that I felt awkward and miserable simply because I was, in fact, awkward and miserable. I believed I felt horrible about myself because I was horrible. I believed that my life as a twelve-year-old sucked because I sucked. It never even occurred to me that any other forces might be at work. The only thing I knew was this: I was the problem. A problem with no solution.

That was years ago. That was before I'd taken any psychology or women's studies classes. That was before *Mean Girls* and *Reviving Ophelia*. That was before it was common knowledge, the way it sort of is today, that girls get absolutely pummeled in middle school and high school. People far smarter than I am have documented how this is true for girls on their journey toward becoming women: That puberty marks the recognition of an unfathomable distance between what women are supposed to be and what girls themselves actually are. That girls make a study of all the ways they fall short. And then they start dieting—or smoking or drinking or vomiting up their dinner. Their grades fall. At the very least, the feisty confidence that little girls have—that my own young daughter has right now as she marches around and investigates everything—disappears. It's a fact of girls' lives.

But I'm not a researcher. I'm just a writer. All I can truly vouch for is what happened to me. And what happened to me was this: sometime around middle school, I got pulled out of my own body. And I've spent the rest of my life trying to get back in.

And I know I'm not the only one. I see it everywhere. Those women who get plastic surgery until they look like Shrinky Dinks? Those women on TV with those quadruple-D breast implants? That old lady who has to wear high-heeled sneakers because years of two-story pumps have irreversibly shortened her Achilles tendons? They all want the same thing I do. We all just want to be able to *go home*—and we've been gone so long, we barely even remember what home looks like. Or, more to the point, what it feels like.

Which brings me back to Duran Duran. Because at times it seems comical to me that during this time of my life, when I was coming to accept that just plain old regular me was nowhere near good enough to deserve the fruits of womanhood, I would obsess over that particular band. A band who featured women in their videos as unlike my possible future self as women could be: rail-thin women in bikinis wrestling in baby oil, or wearing war paint and crawling like panthers through the jungle.

I didn't want to put on a bathing suit, much less a bikini. And I was certainly nowhere close to one of those perfectly made-up, mysterious video ladies who could give Simon such a provocative come-hither look that he'd hop on the back of her moped without even saying hello.

Those women knew what to do with womanhood—or at least they seemed to. In truth, of course, who knows how they felt underneath the makeup and costumes. They knew how to work it and wield it and own it. I didn't even know how to use a curling iron without burning my ears.

And so doesn't that make it even more remarkable, and doesn't it say something so profound about how lovable I am, that even given those crowds of vixens that surrounded them, Duran Duran—*all five!*—chose me? They could have had anyone they wanted. They were being hunted down by half-naked women in the jungle, for Pete's sake! But the person who stole their hearts in the end was the girl in the OP shorts and the Adidas sneakers. With the headgear. And a little bit of acne.

That was sixth grade. In seventh grade, everything changed. We redecorated my bedroom and painted it peach. I got my braces off. One of my best friends defected to a more highly ranked social group, and the other one went with her. My parents started marriage counseling. My grandmother, who I loved like crazy, died suddenly, before we even really knew she was sick. And even though my sister took me to the mall and got me a pair of tapered Guess jeans, I remained a disaster.

That summer, three weeks after losing my grandmother, and as my parents' marriage was dissolving before our eyes, we went to

Greece on a long-planned family vacation. It was an archaeological tour of the Greek islands sponsored by the University of Texas. It was a cruise. And we had done the exact same cruise—though with slightly different stops—two years before, on the exact same boat, in the exact same sea.

But on our second trip, I was no longer the exact same person.

On our first trip, as an eleven-year-old, I had climbed the Acropolis in my braces, boy-short hair and favorite army cap to stare up at the Parthenon in awe. I had sat on the beach at Marathon and tried to visualize the Spartan army coming over the water's horizon in ancient ships. I had marveled over plaster casts of people who had died at Pompeii when Vesuvius erupted. What I remember about that first vacation was learning thing after fascinating thing about one place after another.

Here's what I remember about the second trip: standing on the deck of the ship with my Walkman on, listening to "Save a Prayer" and waiting to be kissed. Because I'd been raised on a steady diet of *The Love Boat,* and if I knew one thing for certain about ships, it was that if you stood on the deck and gazed out at the water long enough, someone would walk out there and kiss you.

By then I was thirteen. I had grown my hair out shoulder length and started wearing blue eyeliner. I'd traded my sneakers for a pair of white Esprit sandals. I'd started wearing bras, I had a whole collection of pastel-colored shirts with shoulder pads, and I was working overtime to leave my former tomboy self behind.

On that second trip we visited some pretty amazing places, like Israel and Turkey and Africa—and I remember my dad complaining about how all his kids wanted to do was stay on the boat and suntan. He made sure to pull us off the boat at every port to visit these places, whether we wanted to go or not. And I do remember seeing them, but I don't remember learning anything about them.

What I recall most from that trip is a Greek sailor named Yiannis, and the fact that one night, when the ship was docked off the coast of the beautiful isle of Lesbos, I snuck down to a lower deck with a bunch of the other teenagers *Dirty Dancing* style to see what the sailors were doing. We found them playing music—Jew's harps, if I remember right—and circle dancing on one of the decks. We stayed long enough that I managed to take my first-ever sip of beer and get kissed before the night was over. I'm not sure how I wound up in an empty hallway with that sailor, but I do remember that not long after his lips touched mine, I pulled back and said, "I don't really know how to do this."

And he just winked at me—and I'm not kidding, here—and said: "I teach."

So what if he was twenty-five and I was barely thirteen? So what if there were a hundred things wrong with that moment? I had suspected for a while that I might never, ever get kissed in my whole life—that *I was not kissable*—and I was indescribably grateful to that cute sailor for proving me wrong. And so, in the cradle of human civilization, with the best and brightest of the University of Texas's archaeology department all around me, what I learned about on that trip was kissing.

Which is fine. Kissing is important, too. Not only because kissing is fun. And not only because I would hold on to the memory of that kiss as a point of pride for many kissless years afterward. But also because when you've lost the ability to be kind to yourself, sometimes you need someone else to step up and do it for you. When your old life disappears from your grasp, you have to grab onto something new. And if it's a Greek sailor with a purple Speedo, so be it.

And if it's world-famous rockers speaking words of love that you write yourself, even better.

Now, looking back, it's a gift to have had those two trips to Greece in the exact years I did. I have a vivid snapshot of the eleven-year-old me, and one just as vivid from two years later. I can compare and contrast. I've got before and after in Technicolor. I can see what I'd lost, and what I was trying so hard to gain.

As for the band members of Duran Duran who existed in my head, they will always have my devotion. For teaching me about how stories offer comfort, and how the imagination can create hope. For seeing me with tender eyes. For proposing marriage over and over again. And, more than anything, for sticking up for me before I had any idea at all how to stick up for myself.

# What Good Is Sitting Alone in Your Room?

## Jon Skovron

Her name wasn't Sally, but that's what I'll call her, in honor of the indomitable Sally Bowles from the Kander and Ebb musical *Cabaret*. If you're not familiar with the story, an earnest young American writer named Cliff comes to 1930s Berlin looking for inspiration, but instead falls in love with a cabaret singer. She loosens him up, and he attempts to clean her up. But in the end, she rejects his offer of a domestic life with house and kids, and opts to continue her decadent, sex- and drug-filled lifestyle, despite the fact that the Nazis have pretty much taken over the country. It doesn't end happily.

The first time I saw *my* Sally was at a local teen production of *Sweeney Todd*. She played Mrs. Lovett, a woman who takes Sweeney Todd's murdered victims and turns them into meat pies that she sells in her shop. Maybe that doesn't sound like the sexiest of introductions, but I was punk rock and pissed off back then. She was brash, loud and dangerous, and I was smitten at first sight.

It was closing night, and I had a bunch of friends in the cast, so I was invited to the party. It was held at Sally's house, which was far enough out into the sticks that roads didn't have names, just route numbers. Sally played the role of charming host, calling everyone "darling" and describing everything in terms of how "marvelous" it was. She was a raucous whirlwind, a bundle of contradictions who seemed to infect everyone around her with her unending effervescence even when she was clearly full of shit. Nobody from the sticks of central Ohio says "marvelous" or "darling."

After several hours of rowdy teenage drinking, things settled down, one thing led to another, and she and I ended up making out on her couch until sometime around dawn. I remember lying there on a rough plaid couch, feeling her warm, soft weight as she slept with her head on my chest. Her glitter makeup, liberally applied to eyes, cheeks and cleavage, was caked on my black T-shirt, and a lock of her burgundy hair was plastered to her full, lipstick-smeared mouth. I looked down at her like she was some strange, exotic bird that I didn't quite know what to do with. I was staunchly anti-drugs and anti-alcohol at the time. If not for my fondness for coffee and cigarettes, I would have been considered straight edge. I was a soldier in the army of Artistic Integrity, and I had no time for decadence, frivolity or the people who promoted them. People like her, in other words. And yet, there I was, staring down into a soft, luscious, moon-shaped face that made it difficult to remember exactly why I was fighting so hard. Maybe I needed to lighten up a bit.

And I did.

Suddenly, I was spending less time at home reading Albert Camus and Edgar Allan Poe, and more time out at coffee shops and concerts. Every weekend she drove an hour out of her way to brave my stepfather's good-natured (if somewhat flirty) teasing and drag me out of my house. I acted like it was a duty I bore grudgingly, but looking back on it, I think it was a pivotal moment in my life. Sally showed me that there was something outside my bedroom and bookshelves. A world filled with fascinating people and fantastic places.

She also supported my passions more than anyone ever had before. She cheered me on at band rehearsals. She urged me to audition for more theater. At every opportunity she challenged me to put myself out there and risk. I quickly realized that if I wanted to hang with this girl, I had to step up my game. So within six months, I was the lead singer in my own band and getting cast as the lead in local theater productions.

I thought she'd be impressed with my successes. And I think, at first, she was. But Sally was not the type to live easily in someone's shadow. Especially after we were both cast in *Godspell,* a 1970s hippie musical version of the New Testament of the Bible. I was Jesus, and she was a chorus girl with only a single solo line. That didn't go over well at all.

Then there was the sex. It wasn't a problem, per se. Only, I was terrified of it. Chalk it up to lectures from my mother about how to please a woman (readers of *Struts & Frets* know what I'm talking about) or my discovery of erotic feminist writer Anaïs Nin too early in life. Or maybe a lot of boys secretly feel this way, and few of us care to admit it. In any case, I was terrified of being deemed "bad" at sex, and even though I thought constantly about sex, I was always too timid to push things very far. For most of our relationship, we never progressed past making out and some groping. I knew that she wasn't a virgin and that it hadn't been entirely her choice. That she had been "sort of raped." So I guess I assumed that she was okay with things not getting too intense in the sex department. I guess I was wrong.

Finally, one hot July afternoon, she showed up at my door in a flowing summer dress, holding a basket.

"Darling, let's have a picnic!" she said.

"Sure," I said.

"But it's so fucking hot out," she said with a pouty face. "And I'm all sunburned. Wouldn't it be so marvelous to have a picnic on the stage?"

"In the theater?" I asked.

"Don't you have keys?"

I did. Because I was the kind of guy who would sneak over during study hall to help the stage manager build scenery. And, of course, smoke lots of cigarettes while we did it.

"Okay," I said.

In truth, it was probably hotter in the un-air-conditioned theater than it was outside. And it was definitely stuffier. But as we sat on the bare wood of the empty stage, I quickly realized it wasn't about that.

We made out for a little while like we usually did. Then suddenly, clothes were coming off. Her hot, sunburned flesh pressed against me and I discovered for the first time the utter joy of the female body. All those Anaïs Nin stories came flooding back into my mind and I was hell-bent on making her orgasm. I'm not sure if I succeeded, but the pleasure of her fingers pulling my hair and her thighs pressed against the sides of my head was enough for me. Then she flipped me on my back. Her soft, wet lips trailed down my neck, chest, stomach, and I was about to receive my very first blow job...when I totally freaked out. Literally, I had a panic attack.

Not the first I'd ever had, and certainly not the last, but possibly the most unfortunate one.

I didn't understand what had happened, but I was fairly sure it was a sign of some serious and possibly unfixable flaw in my manhood. It certainly wasn't anything I was capable of talking about to her, and we parted in an uncomfortable silence. A few days later, she dumped me. Looking back on it, there were many signs before that moment that our relationship had run its course. Perhaps the stage picnic was her last attempt to make it work. Instead, it seemed the final confirmation that it couldn't. I probably don't have to tell you, it gave me a bit of a complex.

A few months later, I heard from a mutual friend that she had dropped out of high school and headed to Europe. A few months after that, I started getting the occasional postcard from her. Nothing specific or revealing. Just lots of "Having a fabulous time in Paris! Frenchmen are so fucking rude!" That sort of thing. I wondered if maybe she missed me. But by that point, I was nearing the end of my senior year and was starting to think about college. I had been accepted at a prestigious acting conservatory in Pittsburgh. I was a soldier for Art once again, and I didn't have time for her dropout, vagabond life.

I went on to my acting training, eating, breathing and sleeping theater all day, every day. I heard rumors about her. That she was back in the States. That she had tattoos. That she was working as a cocktail waitress. That she was working as a go-go dancer. That she was working as a stripper. That she was getting into drugs.... It was like getting points on a line graph that, when you connected the dots, other people seemed to suggest went down, down, down.

But after a year surrounded by nothing but theater professionals, my worldview had expanded considerably. I had experimented with sex and pot a bit and the things I heard about Sally were more intriguing than troubling. I imagined running into her, getting a chance to show her that I wasn't the uptight middle-class boy she thought I was. But I never actually tried to contact her. Instead, I just buried myself in the worlds of William Shakespeare and Samuel Beckett.

One day in the fall of my sophomore year, she called me and said that she was coming to visit. That day. She showed up at my apartment a few hours later looking better than I'd ever seen her, tattoos, piercings and all. She still favored short bobbed haircuts and glitter makeup. She also had with her a big bag of drugs.

It was the first time I had ever done psychedelic drugs. The memory will be fixed in my mind forever as a snapshot of the glorious stupidity of a twenty-year-old. We ate mushrooms in my apartment, choked down with some peanut butter. Then we climbed into my car and headed downtown. We parked just around the time that the drugs started to take hold. For some reason, I thought we needed music, so I brought along an ancient boom box that had been sitting neglected in my backseat. It only had a cassette player, and the only cassette in the car was *Marvin Gaye's Greatest Hits*. So we strolled through the downtown financial district, eyes like eight balls, with "You're All I Need to Get By" blasting from my shoulder. We giggled like crazy people, and imagined ourselves bringing a brief, magical moment of merriment to these grim bankers and accountants.

I fell in love with her all over again. I had been too buried in my studies, I realized. How could I truly hope to be an artist if I didn't experience all that life had to offer? I had a responsibility to drink deeply from the cup of experience. And, of course, the first experience I intended to gulp down was Sally.

We got the idea to go to the Andy Warhol Museum, and somehow, against all odds, we found our way there without a map (and still tripping balls). We smoked a joint for good measure and entered the four-story tribute to the king of Pop Art. I don't remember much about the interior except the Cloud Room. It was filled with strange barnyard sound effects and giant silver balloons that were pushed around by fans built into the floor, ceiling and walls. It was the sort of place that someone in our condition could get utterly lost in for hours. And I am fairly certain we did.

Eventually we managed to get back to our car and find a small, out-of-the-way Indian restaurant in a quiet part of town. We were starting to come down, but the heavy, cold crash was blunted by curry and naan bread. I asked her to sing for me, right there in the restaurant. But she just laughed, pinched my cheek and told me I was so damn cute.

"You could stay for a little while," I said abruptly. "A week or two. Or longer. I know my roommates wouldn't mind."

"Darling, I have to be back to work at the club tomorrow night," she said.

"Right," I said. "The club."

"I'm a stripper," she said brightly.

"That's what I hear," I said.

"It's so much fun," she assured me. "And you make a *ton* of money. I'm like the best pole dancer they've had in years. You should come check me out the next time you're in town."

"Yeah," I said. "Maybe I will."

We both knew I wouldn't.

Sally returned to her dancing pole and I returned to my studies. But once again, Sally had left her mark on me. Long nights of Bertolt Brecht and Anton Chekhov were tempered now by reckless adventures with friends. There was a part of me that still thought about Sally. Not that I had any illusion it would work between us. But I just couldn't let her go completely.

Apparently, neither could she. Sally showed up at my apartment again later that year. But this time she brought three of her coworkers. And instead of shrooms and pot, she brought cocaine. If you've never tried to entertain four coked-up strippers in Pittsburgh, it might sound fun. And there were definitely moments, like late-night impulse nipple piercing. But the nonstop manic, destructive glee with which they attacked the city, combined with the way they treated me rather like their servant or pet, was exhausting. There was something dissatisfied and hungry about them. A hardness beneath their cheer.

Two days later, my food and booze all gone, my apartment trashed, they disappeared as suddenly as they came. I did gain the admiration of many of my friends, but it was difficult to explain to them the strange agony of watching this girl I was still in love with take this journey. I've known women who could handle being a stripper. A single mother who worked her way through college. A dancer who used it to support her avant-garde company. These women tell me that for them, stripping was liberating. But these women had goals. Purpose. Regardless of gender or who's on top, the adult entertainment industry is about power, dominance and exploitation. To navigate its many dangers and pitfalls and come out intact takes inner strength and resilience. As much as I adored her, I wasn't sure Sally had those.

It was two years before I saw her again. I had just graduated from college and was spending a few weeks auditioning for agents and casting directors in Los Angeles before I moved to New York. I heard through the grapevine that Sally was living in Venice Beach, so I decided to look her up. She met me at the door of her apartment, looking seriously strung out and wearing pajamas. Hair cut short and dyed black, no glittery makeup, no smiles. She was stripping at a place on Hollywood Boulevard, she said. She had a stage name now. Betty Boop. I said it suited her. She didn't say much else. Instead, we sat on her bed with her boyfriend, a grim older man covered in tattoos, and watched old episodes of *The Maxx*. After a few hours, I left.

I saw her one more time, about six months later. I was living in one of the seedier parts of Brooklyn, working for a Broadway box office during the day and banging out short literary fiction on a manual typewriter late into the night. A few experiences had turned me away from acting completely, and I had decided to return to my first love, writing.

She called me up out of the blue again (how she always found my phone number, I'll never know). She sounded tired. And tense. She and her boyfriend had just arrived in New York that morning. The place where they were supposed to crash fell through. Could I put them up for a night?

"Of course," I said.

"I'm really sorry, Jon," she said with a gravity and sincerity that took me by surprise. No "darling," no bullshit.

"It's cool," I said, a little unnerved. "Really."

"Thanks," she said.

They showed up a little later, both of them totally sober. And that was good, of course. But there was something missing. This wasn't my Sally Bowles anymore. It wasn't so much that she looked all that different as I looked at her differently. It was that night, at age twenty-three, that I finally relinquished my high school crush. Like a dream, she slipped out of my life early, before I woke up the next morning, and I never saw or heard from her again.

I don't want to give you the idea that I'm sad for Sally, or that I pity her in some way. That would demean her and what she stood for. You see, I was wrong about her not having inner strength. She chose her path and never wavered from it. And she paid a hard price for that. The truth is, it is the Sally Bowles types that bring forth so much of this world's fierce, flawed beauty. I know my life would have been much more drab without her. And for that, she doesn't deserve pity. She deserves gratitude.

# When We Two Parted
## Sheila Kohler

When our teacher asked us, a class of adolescent girls, how many of us would like to marry Heathcliff, all the hands in the class shot up. I imagine if she'd asked us about Mr. Rochester, we would have done the same thing. This, I'm pretty sure, did not augur too well for our futures, our lives as women and wives or even our careers.

My own first marriage, at nineteen, was to a stormy, handsome student of Russian descent whom I had met in Rome, where his mother lived, and where I was studying Italian. One night—we were living in France by then—after declaring undying love for many years, he drank a whole bottle of vodka and confessed that he had fallen in love with another woman. He strode around our bedroom on long legs and pulled at his blond forelock, to confess of his love. "There was nothing I could do!" he said helplessly, as though he had been struck by lightning, beating his breast.

He felt terribly guilty and assured me in agonizing tones that he really loved me, too.

For some reason, I wept for him and for me; I sympathized with his dilemma. It seemed quite possible to me that one might fall in love with someone else, or that was what I told myself as I wandered along the river with its willows—not the weeping kind— in our French garden the next morning. I felt as if I had died, and could not imagine my existence without him. I could not bear the thought of his leaving me and I was ready to do anything to hold on to him.

My mother-in-law, a savvy Southerner, stoked these fires. She kept telling me to treat him as if he had the measles, not to make him feel guilty, and to pretend to be asleep when he came home late at night. All of this added to my religious upbringing, where I had been taught to turn the other cheek.

"I'm just going to say goodbye to her. This is the end," he promised one Christmas holiday, driving off in his green Porsche, scattering pebbles as he went, waving wildly out the window at me, blowing kisses into the wind, and calling out, "I love you! I love you! I love you!" He had given me a sealed letter with his whereabouts, making me promise not to open it except in an emergency. "It will only make you sad," he said. I couldn't resist at some point and found he was in Provence. He had gone to stay at the Colombe d'Or, a beautiful hotel filled with paintings by Picasso and Braque, with a terrace with orange trees and white doves that rose up in the sunset and turned to gold. We had been there together on our honeymoon. Even this I accepted, though of course it broke my heart.

My mother, when I had finally brought myself to tell her what was happening in my marriage, said, "Why don't you throw his clothes out the window and give him a good kick in the balls! What are you doing with this bloodsucker!"—words that come back to me today and make me laugh, thinking of the "*Twilight* phenomenon."

But at the time, I said to her, incensed, "How can you talk like that! He can't help it if he's fallen in love. It could happen to anyone. I'm in love with him, and he loves me. I know he does. He's taught me all I know about life. We've grown up together. We have three children whom we both adore. I can't just leave him!"

"You call that love!" she said in disgust, rolling her eyes at me.

Yet I remained at his side, I hardly dare confess, for ten more years of this. He took to calling me Saint Sheila, while he, losing much of his hair, though he was not much older than I was, took to wearing a large, wide-brimmed hat.

After ten years he told me he had finally managed to leave his lady love. I felt my patience had been justified, until one evening, a few months later, when he came home late again for dinner. I was lying on the bed, reading *Hard Times*—this is true!—and I looked up and said, "If you're going to see your new mistress, why don't you just stay for dinner with her?"

"How did you know?" he said.

A second love affair, with a woman whose name even rhymed with the first one's, was too much even for me. I didn't think one was struck by lightning twice! I left the man and also the country. I came to America, went back to school to study what I had always wanted to study, creative writing, and joined my teenage daughters, who were in college here.

When a friend, who was studying with me, asked if I would like to meet someone new, I asked for a detailed description of the man, being somewhat wary by now. I had more or less come to the conclusion that something in women, or anyway, women of my kind, made us look for these Byronic heroes, these bad boys, these Don Juans. Had not all three Brontë girls devised heroes of this kind? And would I not simply succumb, once again, to one of them, another Heathcliff, however disguised?

Still, lonely in New York with my girls all gone, I was intrigued by my friend's description of the man, a psychiatrist who like myself had children. "A good man," she said. "Do you know what I mean?"

I said I did and hoped that was true. I would have a coffee with him, I consented, and promised myself there would be nothing more than that.

We met in the shadows of a twilit street. The man in question drove up in a sports car, which immediately had me worried, but there was no possibility now of escaping. A good-looking man, slim and well dressed, I could see, and I trembled as he ushered me firmly into a famous coffeehouse in Greenwich Village. We sat down opposite one another. I tried not to look into his dark brown gaze but stared at the reassuring shimmer of white hair. (Surely, Heathcliff would not have such thick white hair?) He asked me about my life. I said as little as possible despite his probing questions. I simply told him my husband had been of Russian origin with a penchant for other women. "He was always very truthful and never lied to me. He told me what was happening. We could always talk," I said, trying to be fair, and warily asked about his life.

He was more forthcoming. He told me his wife of fourteen years, a blue-eyed beauty, was also a truthful person. During the course of their marriage she had told him repeatedly—"every springtime," he said, smiling wryly—"of her lust for other, more strapping (he was, I could see, not particularly tall or muscular) or powerful fellows, though in her case she had had the kindness not to succumb" up until then. She had told him, as my husband had told me, that she did not want to divorce him, that she loved him, even if she was no longer "in love" with him. All she asked was that he would move out of their large Fifth Avenue apartment so that she could bring her lovers in. After all these years she wanted to have the freedom finally to follow her desires.

"So it's not just us women, then?" I said, somewhat surprised by this tale.

"What do you mean?" he asked, and I mentioned the Brontës of my youth and their wild heroes, Mr. Rochester rushing around Thornfield and making poor Jane so jealous, and Heathcliff hanging his wife's pet dog up on a tree by its neck—what my mother had called "those bloodsuckers."

"Well, but think of the great heroines of literature," he said. "They are not so innocent, either. What about rather nasty Emma Bovary with her poor, long-suffering Charles, and her series of lovers, or even adulterous Anna Karenina and her scorn for her husband with the long ears."

"I suppose you're right," I said and looked into his eyes. We both laughed and reached across the table, and I forgot about my resolve to keep this just to coffee.

Still, I think it took both of us some time to trust one another. Certainly, I watched out warily for any signs of infidelity or indifference, and was constantly amazed by and very grateful for acts of kindness: suitcases carried to early-morning trains, or babies (when my children had babies) walked up and down in the steam at midnight when they had colds, dishes washed and dinners cooked, beds made impeccably, and just the daily and constant presence of someone you could count upon to come home on time.

Also, my husband, I think, felt free to argue with me, to voice his opinions and to say what he thought without fear of reprisals. He must have gradually understood that I was the forgiving and constant kind.

After more than twenty years of marriage, I have come to suspect that both our former spouses did us the favor of showing us that the victim is perhaps as responsible as the victimizer. That our guilt, women or men that we might be, often leads us to look for punishment, perhaps even to provoke it. And that in order to find a meaningful partnership, we need to protect the other and also to protect ourselves, which both my husband and I had learned, through much sorrow, to do at last.

# To Sir Anthony, With Love
## Daria Snadowsky

Teen girls are notorious for obsessive celebrity crushes, and back in the mid-nineties I was no different. But instead of plastering my walls with *Tiger Beat* cutouts of Johnny Depp, Christian Slater or Luke Perry, my bedroom doubled as a shrine to none other than...Sir Anthony Hopkins. And unlike most celebrity crushes, which fizzle out, leaving only a pile of crinkled posters in their wake, my Hopkins mania changed my life forever.

I know this sounds disturbing. With all the young and hunky movie stars out there, why would a fourteen-year-old girl lust after a fifty-six-year-old thespian?

Blame it on high school. By the time I survived first semester of freshman year, I'd grown so repulsed by teenage guys that I stopped being attracted to pop-culture heartthrobs who played teenage guys. One of the boys in my grade would snatch the garter snake from biology lab and sneak up with it behind the girls. Another boy used lunch break to thread spaghetti strands up one nostril, down his throat and out of his mouth until both ends of the pasta dangled from each orifice. But the worst was the boy in botany class who impaled his shin on a cactus just to see what would happen—what happened was an open wound that for weeks spontaneously oozed out spines, which he then flaunted like trophies.

To be fair, had I made the effort to talk to these oafs, I might have discovered that their grossness masked hidden depths. But I never made this effort. And it was frustrating because I still pined for a boyfriend, and there was no one even to daydream about.

But that all changed one midwinter Friday evening at the movies!

My mom wanted to see *Shadowlands*, starring Anthony Hopkins as *The Chronicles of Narnia* author C. S. Lewis. I tagged along last minute, expecting a dry biopic about his literary career, but the film actually recounted how C. S. Lewis met and fell in love with his wife, writer Joy Gresham. The story was intoxicatingly romantic, but what struck me most was how Anthony Hopkins's portrayal exemplified all the attributes the boys in my school seemingly lacked: Maturity. Dignity. Chivalry. Eloquence. Accomplishment. Charisma. Wit. Sensitivity. Loyalty. And when you mix all that together, you get SEXINESS, irrespective of age. (The British accent didn't hurt, either.) By *Shadowlands'* end credits, I was besotted, and that weekend morphed into a full-out Anthony Hopkins binge fest.

On Saturday I went to see *The Remains of the Day* and nearly swooned when Anthony Hopkins stared ravenously at Emma Thompson. That same evening I rented *Bram Stoker's Dracula* and shrieked jealously when he kissed Winona Ryder on the lips. Later that night I watched our VHS copy of *The Silence of the Lambs* and all but melted when he grazed Jodie Foster's finger through his cage bars. (Needless to say, I overlooked the psychotic aspect of his character.) Then on Sunday I caught *The Bounty* on cable and barely noticed his costars Daniel Day-Lewis, Liam Neeson and a shirtless Mel Gibson—crushes are monogamous.

Yes, of course I was aware Anthony Hopkins was only acting in his films and that I might not even like him if we met in real life. But that's the whole point of having a celebrity crush: you can project all your fairy-tale illusions on a superhuman persona and fabricate a perfect, consequence-free relationship precisely because it is unattainable. I knew my make-believe life with him would serve as an ideal distraction from my humdrum nonlife in ninth grade. Also, it just felt so good to really *want* somebody. As Anthony Hopkins as C. S. Lewis says in *Shadowlands,* "The most intense joy lies not in the having, but in the desiring." And *desire* I did.

In the weeks that followed, I pored over and practically memorized Anthony Hopkins's authorized biography, and then his *un*authorized biography. I leafed through every entertainment magazine available for his photos to paste in my scrapbook. Employees of movie memorabilia shops started recognizing me as I regularly searched their inventory for production stills to display in my room. My local interlibrary loan clerks remained busy fulfilling my requests for his more obscure films. And I stayed up until the early hours to tape his late-night talk show appearances. Remember, these were the days of dial-up internet, before online auctions, fan sites and video sharing became widespread, so hard-core celebrity crushers were forced to be self-sufficient.

I suppose I should've foreseen that telling my classmates about the new object of my "desire" would result in social suicide, but it seemed wrong to keep something so special a secret. As the old cliché goes, I wanted to scream my love from the rooftops, which, in high school terms, meant covering all my notebooks and text-books with pictures of him and raving about his movies to anyone who would listen. Not surprisingly, I was soon branded the school wacko, and a week rarely passed without someone posting a vulgar prank note on my locker saying, "Oh, Anthony, do me, baby!" and "Eat me, Hannibal!" But I didn't care—being "wacko" was a small price to pay for feeling the most alive I'd ever been.

What I *never* could've foreseen, though, was how my crush's films would expose me to extraordinary treasures I might not have appreciated otherwise: *A Doll's House* introduced me to playwright Henrik Ibsen. *Chaplin* gave me my first taste of silent cinema. *Howards End* led me to the masterpieces of author E. M. Forster. And as in any great romance, I felt inspired to create. I filled an entire drawing pad with sketches of him, which weren't half bad. I also wasted a whole floppy disk with odes in verse to him, which were really, *really* bad. Brace yourself for a sampling of some irre-deemable couplets where I gushed about his body:

> *His capped teeth—pillars of a great stately home.*
> *His fleshy nose—a pink capillaried dome.*
> *His blue eyes—dual oceans defying metaphor.*
> *His thick neck—embroidered with wrinkles galore.*
> *His limp, stubby arms—inviting indeed.*
> *His stout, agile calves—of an eccentric steed.*
> *Those liver spots that dot that noble brow.*
> *Those nerdy eyeglasses that seem just right, somehow.*

By my sophomore year, it finally began to irritate me that my crush was so one-sided. I wasn't deluded enough to imagine

Anthony Hopkins would ever care to know me, let alone requite my affections. But after everything I'd done because of him, I figured I deserved some small recognition of my existence *by* him. Therefore, I resolved to send him my best drawings for his December 31 birthday in the hopes he'd personally write me back. Thus commenced my quest to hunt down his home mailing address.

But after six weeks and ten times as many phone calls to movie studios, production companies, talent agencies and property records offices in both the U.S. and the U.K., the most I could scrape up was a fan mail address, which would not do. I didn't want my drawings to suffocate under heaps of other fan letters that *maybe* would be glanced at by an assistant who then *maybe* would respond with a form thank-you card that *maybe* would contain a hastily scribbled autograph. I wouldn't be satisfied unless I received something meaningful and unique from him, something that would unquestionably demonstrate that, for at least a second or two, I commanded Sir Anthony Hopkins's full attention and perhaps even made him smile. And since time was ticking away, I was left with little choice but to enter shameless harassment mode.

With the help of 4-1-1, I compiled a list of phone numbers of Anthony Hopkins's noncelebrity industry friends, whom I'd read about in various trade publications. I'd call, identify myself as a fan, and request to send them my letter to pass along directly to the great man. As I predicted, most of these people promptly hung up on me, but eventually I reached a kind, patient gentleman in Pacific Palisades, California, who answered, "Sure! Send it over." *Then* he hung up on me. I had no reason not to believe him, so I placed my drawings in a hard manila envelope, affixed to it postage stamps bearing the word *LOVE*, mailed it out and waited.

But nothing happened.

By spring semester, I was resigned to the whole project being a bust, and I berated myself for presuming I could earn the admiration of one of the most celebrated dramatic artists of the twentieth century. But then one February afternoon when I'd come home from school, more than a year after Anthony Hopkins's performance as C. S. Lewis shook me to the core, I received a letter with an unfamiliar return address and a Queen Elizabeth stamp. I'd already given up hope of ever hearing from him, so it honestly didn't occur to me that he could be the sender. I apathetically tore open the envelope and yanked out the enclosed sheet of paper, which read:

*Dear Daria,*

*It was very kind of you to remember my birthday and send me a card and those sketches. You are obviously very talented, although I hope my nose isn't quite so bulbous! Thank you for taking so much trouble.*

*Yours sincerely,*
*Sir Anthony Hopkins*

The next two hours passed as a euphoric blur, and I suddenly understood the expression "walking on air." I just kept thinking, *Anthony Hopkins wrote to* me! *He touched* this *piece of paper! How adorable that he thought I made his nose too bulbous!* I must have reread that letter a thousand times. It was *everything* I could have wanted in a reply: personal, genuine, and one of a kind. At long last, I had something concrete to show for all my hope and labor, and for a brief moment in human history, my dream man became real. Mission accomplished.

Anticlimactically enough, however, my love cooled shortly thereafter. I still saw all his films and collected his newspaper clippings, but it was more out of inertia than infatuation. There just wasn't anything to yearn for anymore, and I recalled that line from *Shadowlands,* which started it all: "The most intense joy lies not in the having, but in the desiring." Well, I "had" what I "desired" in the form of his letter, and now that I'd communicated with the authentic Sir Anthony Hopkins, the fanciful Sir Anthony Hopkins no longer delivered the same escapist excitement. (Also, the boys at school were getting cuter.) So my imaginary love affair had come to an end, but as I mentioned at the beginning, this differed from other celebrity crushes because it affected the rest of my life. I wouldn't realize how, though, until my senior year.

It was deep into college application season, and I was competing for a merit scholarship to one of my top-choice universities. They required an extra essay about something significant I'd done, but when I reflected on the previous three years of high school, I couldn't come up with anything to write about that wasn't totally unremarkable. I instantly regretted my fifteen-month-long celebrity crush.

How could I have wasted all those hundreds of precious hours on something so pointless? While my peers were volunteering for Habitat for Humanity and conducting science fair experiments, I was watching *Legends of the Fall* yet again and envisioning Anthony Hopkins and me riding back on a Montana ranch.

But it wasn't a waste. And it wasn't pointless. Okay, by most standards it was, but it meant a great deal to *me.* My crush helped me through a particularly unbearable period in high school.

I learned a lot about film, art and literature that was undeniably enriching. And for the first time in my life, I was truly passionate about something, which is an unbeatable feeling.

"So, write your essay about that," my mom advised me during dinner one evening. "What's important is being passionate, not what you're passionate about."

"No, it wouldn't work," I droned. "The whole thing's too bizarre, and I'm embarrassed by it now."

"Still, it's not every day a teenager tracks down such a famous man in the manner you did."

"But who would ever care that I once went gaga over the guy who played Dr. Lecter?"

Then my dad interjected, "This isn't about idol worship. It's about overcoming brick walls. You set a goal for yourself, and you went after it. Isn't that all those admissions people care about, anyway?"

"Well...maybe," I conceded, the idea growing on me. "And one thing's for sure—I would definitely stand out from all the other applicants."

"Exactly," Mom and Dad said in unison.

So I went to work at my computer, likening my quest for Anthony Hopkins's acknowledgment of me to a Greco-Roman myth. I equated my ardor for him to that of the Argonauts seeking the Golden Fleece. I compared my nightmare image of his mountain of fan mail burying my drawings to a whirling Charybdis of oblivion. I even quoted the last line of Alfred, Lord Tennyson's "Ulysses" when describing my determination for our two souls to cross paths: "To strive, to seek, to find, and not to yield."

I freely admit it was over the top. But it was also original and completely heartfelt. And it must have been effective, because a few months later I received some other mail, this time informing me I'd won a full ride for all four years.

When I moved into my dorm room that fall, I immediately hung the Anthony Hopkins letter above my desk. The "conversation starter" value was priceless. More importantly, though, it functioned as a constant reminder that harebrained fantasies can beget Herculean feats, and that reaching for the stars (literally or figuratively) is the first step to catching one. Relentlessly crushing over a movie actor may very well have been "wacko," but isn't wackiness an essential ingredient for all creative endeavors? If nothing else, it provides unusual material for scholarship essays. And truthfully, it wouldn't have made a difference had Anthony Hopkins never answered me. I still could have penned that essay, and this essay, about how deeply I felt and how hard I tried, which is what really matters when pursuing a dream. Sir Anthony Hopkins and I may not have lived happily ever after, but my crush adventure proves that, in one way or another, passion pays off.

# It Never Was, Not Really

## Steve Almond

Did I stalk Lauren Chang? I would say no. True stalking requires more than an exuberance for humiliation. You've got to be committed to the squirmy pleasures of intimidation and willing to breach the perimeter of criminal intent. I'm not courageous or organized enough for all that. So I've made a project—a rather poor project—of sticking to suburban misbehavior.

Nonetheless, I will not claim with any assurance that I did *not* stalk Lauren Chang. The question seems best posed to Lauren Chang herself, whose precise whereabouts I will mention right now I do not possess. But before I delve further into this business, I will mention two earlier affairs, which to my mind foreshadowed the appearance of Madame Chang in my life.

The first was with a certain Muffy Ross. Her name wasn't really Muffy. (Her name, like all others in this account, has been changed.) But she had the Muffy spirit, essentially haughty with bouts of girlish enthusiasm, and she had the Muffy look, as if she'd just stepped off a tennis court. I'd met her at a party held high up in the hills above our suburb, a place where the driveways were a mile long. I recognized her immediately as someone born above my station and I spent a miserable month or so trying to woo her, the culmination of my efforts being a date at a Stickney's Restaurant to which I rode my bicycle about five miles in summer, thus sweating through my one dressy sweater, which was (Lord forgive me, I was fourteen) black angora. Perhaps a year later, Muffy walked into the ice cream shop where I worked with a tall, handsome suitor. He smiled, showing me his ten thousand teeth, all of them white.

A few years later I wooed Ellie, another highborn maiden. We sucked face a few times and snuck into the town swimming pool at midnight, where we tossed about like ugly dolphins. Then I came around to take her on a proper date. At the end of the evening, I kissed her, transferring from my tongue to hers a wild cherry Life Saver, a piece of lingual guile I must have considered the height of sangfroid. She responded by letting out a small shriek and casting the offending candy on the ground. Later, Ellie shipped off to Harvard and I went to visit her for the weekend. She abandoned me in her room as quickly and courteously as she could. I immediately located her journal and was rewarded with an entry detailing the recent loss of her virginity. She described making love as like "riding down a mountain." There was a small line drawing of her descending a mountain on skis. That night, I slept at the foot of her bed—like Ruth from the Bible, only horny and bitter.

I mooned over both these women for months after it was clear they wanted nothing to do with me. My allegiance was rooted in absurd, ulterior notions: that Muffy would eradicate my class anxieties, Ellie my intellectual deficiencies. Mostly, I needed to feel the sting of my own inadequacies, to which I had grown quite attached over a course of a long oily adolescence.

But what of Lauren Chang? We met our first year in college. I dated a friend of hers for about two minutes. It took about a week for me to realize Lauren was the one, but it was already too late. She was dating a soccer player. I was a soccer player, too, but the scrawny, ambivalent kind.

What did I like about Lauren? She was beautiful, though not in any obvious way. Her two front teeth were slightly too large, which accentuated the bow of her mouth. She was poised. Most of all, she was funny. It was not something I expected, owing to her poise, owing to her clothes, which were neat and clean, right on the cusp of preppy.

I admired her from afar for most of college. We drove up to Williams one time to watch her boyfriend play soccer. I had quit the team by then and was calling the games on the college radio station. Lauren was sly, but not in the mean collegiate way. More as if she recognized the absurdity of our circumstance, the idea that we'd take ourselves seriously at such a tender age. She said things that made me laugh. I can't remember what, but I remember marveling at her assurance and her insight.

Toward the end of senior year, my housemate Winnie told me Lauren and her guy had split. She slept over a few nights later. I could hear them gabbing away downstairs. I lay on my bed in a riot of want. Then I stood up and stripped off my shirt and did fifty quick push-ups and walked downstairs and stood in front of the fridge near Winnie's room. I suppose I could have greased up my triceps, but that would have seemed excessive.

The girls had been drinking wine. Thankfully. They beckoned to me. I ambled into Winnie's room and pretended I was embarrassed to be caught with my shirt off—little old me—and ran back upstairs to cover my naked self.

Anyway, it worked. An hour later, as I lay on my bed simmering in illicit wishes, a soft knock sounded. There was Lauren in a long T-shirt and not much else. Miracle of miracles! "I decided to stay over," she said. "But there's no room in Winnie's bed. Is there room in yours?"

It is now time to disclose a *possibly indicting fact:* I was, at this particular point in time, dating another woman. Rather seriously.

I stared at my pathetic twin mattress. I stared at Lauren's shimmering legs. "Yeah," I said.

So we climbed into bed together and lay there whispering in the dark. But here's something weird: I didn't sleep with Lauren that night. I didn't even make out with her. Was this because I was dating another woman? No. It was because Lauren had bad breath. As I think back on who I was at that point in my life, my essential depravity, I'm amazed that this would have been a deal breaker.

But I can see now that I was already harboring certain fantasies about Lauren Chang, about her feminine infallibility. My girlfriend at the time was a tall, histrionic sort, prone to flowing gowns and sighs. I didn't like her very much, but everyone said she was beautiful, so I didn't have much choice.

I am almost certain that it was my rejection of Lauren that caused her to pursue me, inasmuch as she did, over the next few weeks. The culmination was just a few weeks before graduation. We wound up at her place, with Winnie, watching some dumb video. The movie ended. Winnie—with a doubtful glance at us—took off. Lauren disappeared into the bathroom and returned in boxer shorts, her mouth smelling of toothpaste. She led me into the bedroom.

I've tried to remember many times what it was like to make love to Lauren Chang. All I remember is that she gave me a condom to put on and told me to be gentle and that it felt really good—which is sort of a gimme, I guess—and that I spent a lot of my energy trying not to come (also a gimme) and sucked at her neck hard enough to give her a small, dark hickey. Then it was over and she went to sleep and I gazed at her face for four hours straight.

At five in the morning, I got up and slipped into my clothes. I was too nervous to sleep, as I had a girlfriend already and so was in the wrong morally, and I wanted to get home so that Winnie and my other housemates (who knew my girlfriend) would wake to find me at home.

Lauren stirred. "Where are you going?" she said.

"I should take off," I said. "I've got this paper to finish."

Lauren regarded me with a sort of drowsy consternation. Her body lay curled beneath a thin sheet. "Don't worry about it," she said softly. "Stay here. We can have breakfast." She paused. "My housemates don't care."

And here we have arrived at the moment my memory has deemed pivotal. Lauren Chang lay abed in all her poise, in all her soft skin, the purple light of dawn gathered around her, calling out to my maturity, gently urging me to surrender my ridiculous anxieties, my guilt, my dishonesty, the excuses I found in nearly every arena of my life to not reach for what I truly wanted. She was trying to tell me that I *could* have what I wanted, but only if I showed the proper courage.

Was this really what Lauren Chang was thinking or feeling? Of course not. It is the sort of horseshit manufactured, over many years, by the wishes we knit into regret. What Lauren was thinking was probably more along the lines of: *Come back to bed, you idiot.* Or: *Howzabout you don't make me feel like a slut?*

The bottom line is I left. I walked across campus in a cloud of manufactured decency. Yes, I'd cheated on my girlfriend. But it didn't count, because I'd left before the cock crowed. Right?

By eight that morning, I had decided to split up with my girl-friend, so as to pursue my destiny with Lauren Chang. This plan lasted until approximately 9:30 a.m., at which point I spotted Lauren emerging from the campus post office. She was wearing a turtleneck to cover the hickey. I recall her expression as falling somewhere between remorse and full-fledged dread.

I assumed this was to be attributed to my hasty and ungallant retreat. She was hurt, you see. She thought she meant more to me than that. I wanted to explain to her right there that I was her man, she was my woman, all we needed now was a sunset into which to ride off. I might even have tried to hug her.

But if I did, she didn't want to hug. And if I didn't, it was because I realized that she didn't want to hug.

There was a month left in my college career, and I spent most of that time distancing myself from my girlfriend—though not actu-ally breaking up with her—and attempting to engineer a reunion with Lauren.

There was some senior party on the eve of graduation; she looked breathtaking in a strapless gown. I kept trying to lure her outside so I could suck on her neck some more, but she wanted to dance. She was so casual, casual to the point of maybe not really giving that much of a shit about me. But it was my belief some-thing sacred had transpired between us. I was possessed by the thought that we would be together.

That summer, I moved to Phoenix for an internship. I got a postcard from Lauren. She was driving across country and would visit in August. I read this postcard over and over, searching the neat script for secret signs of devotion. My entire summer seemed to pivot around this visit. Something momentous was going to happen.

But I remember almost nothing of the visit itself. I took Lauren to my favorite teriyaki place and listened to everything she said about the job she was going to take in Boston as a consultant. I kept looking at her—at how lovely she was, at her poise—and hoping she would look back at me, searchingly, wantingly, as she had before. I was staying in a lousy dorm with a roommate, but I made him clear out for the night so Lauren and I could be together.

She calmly set up a sleeping bag on the floor.

"You don't have to do that," I said, or words to that effect. But she didn't answer. I couldn't get her to acknowledge my desire and what it meant.

It was obvious what was going on, that she wasn't interested, that our night together was a one-time thing, a fling she'd indulged in out of errant loneliness, not some exalted sense of possibility. But I couldn't see it.

None of us can when we're in this situation. I kept clinging to the fantasy that she wasn't quite ready to acknowledge her desire yet, that I still had a shot, though the larger fantasy had nothing to do with her. It had to do with my own abject needs. If I could be good enough for her, I could be good enough for myself. Such is the absurd fantasy that animates all our crushes, young or old.

And this is the direct line that might be drawn from Muffy to Ellie to Lauren, that each of them revealed, or activated, some node of self-loathing, some unconsciously nurtured symptom of my basic unlovability. How we long for this sort of misery, we children of neglect!

A few months later, I would travel to Boston to visit Lauren, yet again. She lived in Beacon Hill, and I remember getting my rental car hopelessly lost on those quaint cobbled streets. I was sweating when I arrived and I reached to embrace her but there was nothing for me to hold on to but a few polite bones.

Later, at dinner, I asked her if we might ever get together again. "I just want it to be like it was before," I said, or words to that effect. It was what I'd said to Ellie years earlier, on a bridge overlooking the Charles, and Lauren's answer (though my memory has been kind enough to expunge the exactitudes) ran along the lines of Ellie's: "There never was a before, Steve. Not really." I stared at my rigatoni, the marinara like drying blood, and we staggered through the rest of the night.

That should have been it. I should have walked away. But instead, I stored Lauren away in the back of my mind, as a reminder of what I didn't deserve. If only I had stayed the morning, made her breakfast, mustered the assurance she needed...life would have been perfect.

Not long afterward, Lauren wrote me a long, funny letter, the tail end of which mentioned a new friend, a man, about whom I knew (and know) nothing, but whose image nonetheless took clear shape in my mind. He was an athlete—varsity lacrosse—tall and blond and rangy, a bit preppy, strong jaw, confident and good with money. I was describing myself, of course, the exact guy I wasn't and couldn't be, and why Lauren hadn't chosen me.

It took me two decades to rid myself of Lauren Chang, to realize that her rejection had as little to do with me as my obsession had to do with her. These were mostly lonely years, during which

I punished all the women who showed the poor judgment to love me back. I didn't want them, of course. I even managed to fall in love with a young woman who looked a bit like Lauren and to have sex with her with a delicious and disastrous abandon until she, too, dumped me.

The crucial ingredient in love is self-recognition. I spent a lot of time figuring that out, often with paid help from professionals. And it finally took root in time for me to marry and have a family before it was too late. I don't believe in God, but I thank the universal spirit for this—and the paid help, and my wife.

Lauren led just about the life I figured she would. Married in her twenties, had three lovely children and settled, curiously, in the city where I grew up. She met my father not long ago, at a political fund-raiser. And when he told me about this meeting ("Oh, Steve, I met an old friend of yours"), I could feel the old thrum of adrenaline, the grand *If Onlys* we use to measure our discontents.

The feeling lasted about a minute. Then my daughter, who was in the other room, shouted to me that she wanted to hear a story, something about herself and the power of magic. I was only too happy to oblige.

# Red All Over

## Tara Bray Smith

Had there been sexting or IMing or Facebook in 1985, undoubt-
edly I would have confessed my love for Shaun M. there,
perhaps squeezing it in beside the anonymous penises of
Chatroulette, but what was available for the expression of sweet
hot-teenaged lust "back then"—indeed, what was *assigned* (it
was called journaling, and it would do for the unburdening of
a secret sentence or two)—were those black-and-white Mead
composition books, "marble" covered, sewn, ruled in chaste
light blue. To fill the Mead with one's thoughts, in handwriting
as large as possible, was a semester's English homework. We
bought them at our high school's bookstore, outside of which
Kimo Higgins and Eric Heneghan loafed, hollering *"Fat corn!"*
to anyone who passed by. *Fat corn!*—a private joke, something
about a wrestling camp in Iowa. Such were the metaphors of
adolescence. They might have given me an idea of what was on

a sixteen-year-old boy's mind, but I was fourteen and my heart was as tender as a frog.

I wrote earnest compositions in those black-and-white books for Mr. Dunlap, my freshman year English teacher, about my parents' divorce, wanting to be bulimic as a route to popularity, questions of aesthetics (*I wonder if I should wear my muumuu tomorrow. Or should I wear something else? What do you think? I think a muumuu tomorrow would be awsum*). And starting in April or May, as we prepared for the epic beach tug-of-war that would determine the winner of the class Olympics, I began to write about love. It was the mid-eighties. I was on an island in Hawaii, twenty-five hundred miles from the nearest continent, and the only person I'd been in love with was Magnum, P.I., and that was because he looked like my dad.

*Hi, journal. Well, these are the last ten pages of journal from my freshman year. I'm really stoked 'cause I like Shaun. He is really nice, and funny, and cute, and sweet, and shy.*

There is nothing more shameful than trying to express one's adolescent longings in words on paper—except maybe falling deeply and madly in love with someone who really only liked you for a few weeks. *Shaun M.* His friends called him Murf. A mutual friend introduced us by way of a series of check boxes: yes, no, sort of. We declared our intentions in ballpoint (*you're cool*) and at a Saturday dance, somewhere between "White Lines (Don't Do It)" and "In the Air Tonight," found a dark corner and started our delirious march around the bases. His lips flubbered and sucked; I ran my tongue over his teeth and tickled the roof of his mouth and licked at its corners and he kissed behind my ears and down my neck and put his hand in my shirt and I snapped the waistband of his BVDs and I wanted it all to never, ever stop.

I was in ninth grade; Shaun, a junior of incipient slacker taste and dirty blond hair just long enough to get into his (thickly lashed, Bambi-wide) eyes. Perhaps he wanted to do more than just kiss? He always seemed to be getting out from under me, but I was mesmerized by him and could not think of much else to do when we were together but put my bruised and chapped mouth on his and close my eyes and hang on, like a barnacle on a ship.

*Shall I tell you a little about Mr. Shaun M.? Okay, I will. Let's start with his classes. A period he has chemistry. B period he has free. C period he has Japanese. D period Comp II. E period he has lunch, and F period algebra. Finally, G period he has U.S. history with Kandel. Now I will progress to his friends. He likes Scooter, Paul, Brooks (his roommate), Ian and etc. He hates Scott McKay, Melissa McKay, Johnette and Paul Muller. His work-crew job is dinner scraping, and he is an alternate at Mr. Tooman's table. He is originally from Sydney, Australia, but when he was three, he moved to Papua New Guinea. He has a sister named Skye and he almost died when he was a child. I don't know his favorite color, or number, but I'll find it out!*

First love is bound to crush you, perhaps in my case by an abundance of detail. We went together after that, though prom had already passed—my date had been the French-Chinese son of an astronomer who asked me why I made so much noise when I Frenched—and only a month remained of the semester. I tried to waylay Shaun as often as possible in those last weeks, my favorite spot being behind the chapel around midmorning. The reverend was known to tipple and Shaun and I could maul each other there in the tall grass, the shade of eucalyptus trees dappling his khakis. We got into each other's pants, gave each other hickeys, dry humped. Our boarding school, Hawai'i Prep—what a brand!—had been built on a former cattle ranch whose stubbly fields stretched into the clouds. If you weren't on the beach bus headed down to Hapuna on a Sunday with your best friend to spend the day comparing upper thigh fat, you could hike across the fields to Anna's Pond, into which a waterfall literally cascaded and where our school's not insubstantial stoner crowd was rumored to hunt for mushrooms in the cow patties. One weekend I entreated Shaun to hike over but the gate had been locked or maybe he just wanted to go back to his dorm to play video games.

*I guess the worst thing about the whole relationship is that all I can think about is having sex with him. I guess that's a little kinky, and I shouldn't write it in my journal, but I'm absolutely serious. I really want to have sex with Shaun M., of all people! I suppose it sounds pretty stupid, but it's absolutely true, that's what I want. I don't know if I will, because that is a whole different story. I'd be too scared of becoming pregnant.*

(Here Mr. Dunlap annotated in his slanting, adult hand, "Probably a good idea.")

Why did I confess so much? There was the prolonging of passion by recalling it, and the fantasy of controlling the future by listing all the possible ways it could play out. And the English teacher required it. (I told Mr. Dunlap I loved him, too, in an entry/Oscar speech: "I guess this isn't called the best writing I've ever done, but it's the most truthful. I love you. And thanks.") In any case, I went along, scribbling every morning in the open-air hallways of the classroom buildings, calls of "Fat corn!" ricocheting off the actual lava-rock walls.

Hawai'i Prep was built among the foothills of an old volcano, long judged extinct, but who knew about eternity? School ended; the journal in which love proliferated disappeared somewhere—misplaced during the divorce, I assumed. Shaun's class won the tug-of-war. I cried. I went to Honolulu to say goodbye to him and his fellow PNGers at the airport. His two best girlfriends, Nikki and Kara—jaunty, freckled tomboys with small boobs and asymmetrical haircuts—had rented a cheap hotel room and we all got plastered on Bartles & Jaymes. I wanted Shaun to come into the bedroom, where we could slide around on the polyester bedspread, but he stayed on the balcony, drinking his Foster's. I had the feeling he was making fun of me—the old lady!—but I couldn't leave the bed in case he wanted to kiss. After the moon had risen and disappeared and we'd all had enough strawberry hooch to color our mouths scarlet, I jumped on the foldout facing the lanai, trashed. The lights of the booze cruises off Waikiki lurched. I was full of rage and frustration, lust, and a longing that I was only beginning to understand as terrifying. And I had not found out his favorite number.

Girls are like melting Popsicles the first time they fall in love. We never reconstitute. I have never been in love like I was with Shaun, and I'm married. I wrote to him that summer, of course. My stepmother and father had finished their divorce and I was staying with Dad in a one-bedroom converted garage in Honolulu, sleeping on the sofa next to the kitchen, both of us bachelors of a sort. He worked at a hotel; I sold dolphin charms at the Honolulu aquarium and took care of babies at DeDe's N-Shape, an aerobics studio down the hill. I wrote Shaun faithfully, on whale stationery pilfered from the aquarium gift shop. I sent him Billabong shorts for his birthday; he sent a letter or two back. A month into the isolation I saved up enough to call him in Port Moresby. Not much to say, at least from his side.

"Hello?"

"Hey."

"I miss you so much!" (Where was my shame? My pride?)

"Dude. No worries. Fat corn!"

The call lasted nine minutes and cost forty dollars. I cried at least a day or two after it.

When school began again, I had grown my hair and lost fifteen pounds through DeDe's ministrations to tighten my *okole*. Did Murf notice? He said he liked my hair before. Classes started; he broke up with me. He told me to think about him like he was going on a trip. Maybe he'd be back! A few days later he started going with Lia Jett, a new freshman who had once been in a Stevie Nicks video, playing a gothic street urchin. I couldn't blame him totally. Lia had wispy blond hair and a removable clear retainer. Her mother inhabited a compound somewhere near Captain Cook and was rumored to be married to a man from Hollywood. In my sophomore year journal—on to Mr. Bryson—I cataloged the hideous pain of being a scorned woman.

*White lines going through my mind—and all the while*
*I think of you. White lines a vision dream of passion—*
*Rang Dang Diddy di Dang di Dang. Cause white lines.*
*Go away. Freeze.*

I had admirers: Dave V. (Snaggletooth). Another S., who took me to Maui, also with the bi-level haircut but pale-eyed and thin-lipped, and he said "dude" a lot. A tall and hale British chap from Saudi Arabia walked me from classes to my dorm every day. He would have carried my books were the eighties only slightly more square. He gave me a St. Christopher's medal on a silver chain and I wore it with wounded fury while Lia and Shaun dragged on. When they broke up, he went after another flyaway blonde, Dayna, a transplant from Iowa who ran cross-country with her bronze ice Wet 'n' Wild tucked into her bra strap. It became a small fad.

Other girls took pity on me because I could be counted on to weep in my dorm room or at house parties. At one I found myself downstairs in a guest bedroom, blubbering, Shaun on a porch above me, visible through a seventies-era bubble sunroof. I had a perfect view of his long legs and the blond leg hair shimmering in the late-afternoon sun. I sobbed so theatrically that eventually someone—it may even have been the boy himself—came down to check on me. I feigned sleep. So I was faking it a little. Something was real in all the heaving; I just can't remember what.

The year dragged on; he listed my initials in his final yearbook entry *(Thanks to:)*, occasioning more weeping. Formaldehyde drifted out of Conley's biology classroom in thick puffs. We graduated from frogs to cats. They lay stacked on each other in the biology freezer, our names dangling off paws like Christmas tags. Shaun was planning a party with the other S., their invitation a Budweiser label Shaun had drawn, "Fat corn!" somehow worked in. The party would be down at the beach, a few days after graduation. I had started dating the son of a veterinarian by then and I'd bring him, a sweet brown-haired boy who knew several horses by name.

It might have been graduation day itself. We were in the gym, risers full, the entire school gathered, and I walked in wearing one of my stepmother's dresses—I think it was polka-dotted—head high. There may have even been a hat. I was nearly sixteen, publicly over him. I had, Gloria Gaynor style, survived.

My tall British guy, the gentle giant who had given me the St. Christopher's medal, walked up to me in front of the entire school and handed me my freshman year journal, the one I thought I had lost the previous year, the one in which I averred, "All I can think about is having sex with him," and "I guess that's a little kinky." "I think this is yours," he said. He looked pained. For a year my Mead had made the rounds, in and out of boys' dorm rooms, coming back to me with the mistakes in Shaun's schedule corrected: "D period, lunch, E, Comp II."

There was nothing to do but take it, assume my place in the risers and stand to sing the school anthem. I stopped writing for a while after that.

Love and shame and words on a page: they've never parted for me. It all got hopelessly scrambled the day an entire school read my diary and even now writing induces the cringing, smiting, inflaming, occasionally breathtaking desire to bare everything while also knowing that doing so will smash me—much like love.

Boys continued reading my diaries; I continued writing in them. Twice lovers have snuck a peek, woe to them. When I married and moved into my husband's apartment, I took them all, the notebooks, the spiral-bounds, the pink padded one under lock and key—starting with the Mead 1985. I didn't have much else—some clothes, my books, my flatiron. For a few minutes, packing, I thought I'd lost them in a previous move and I scrambled through twenty years of reused cardboard boxes and all my sundry, worthless crap till my hands bled. I've told my husband never to read them; he wouldn't like what he'd find. (There are pages inscribed top to bottom with the word *fuck*. Perhaps I was trying to get at all its meanings?) Which is the truth, as far as I am able to determine, about both diaries and the human heart.

Love is perpetually ashamed, secret, and very often unreadable. According to Facebook, where we can keep track of each other's scores and losses, movie-star doppelgänger, breakfast habits, recent travel and evening plans, I find Shaun happily married to a fellow Aussie, father to a sweet-looking baby, still grinning in a T-shirt, still with that charming, floppy hair. Far too shy to friend him, I prowled around his public profile for a while—one particular chamber of this frog's heart being sealed up forever.

# Consequently Yours
## Laurie Faria Stolarz

The first time I spoke to him was in college. I was sitting in the campus café, working on a last-minute assignment for marketing class, when this boy walked in, took a seat across from me at my table, and pushed my books to the side.

"Hey," he said. "I'm Peter."

I knew who he was. We were in a writing class together that semester, plus I'd seen him around campus. But since we didn't have any of the same friends in common, *and* since we both sat at polar opposite sides of the classroom, we didn't exactly have the occasion for conversation.

Until that afternoon.

After an exchange of a few paltry pleasantries, Peter looked straight into my eyes and asked me where I got my inspiration. He was talking about an essay I'd written, one that the professor had asked me to share with the class.

"I'm sort of fascinated by the choices people make," I told him. "And by how the consequences of those choices play out down the road, even several years later."

"So does that mean that my decision to come and sit with you just now will have a long and lasting consequence?"

The question made me laugh. After which, there was more talking and laughing. Three whole hours of it. *Three hours* of us swapping stories about our hometowns (he was from the suburbs; I was more of a city girl), sharing what we wanted out of life (I dreamt of becoming a writer, while he had an interest in pursuing law), and comparing our quirkiest part-time jobs (I once had a job making boob-shaped mugs at a ceramics studio, while he dressed as a fish to wait tables at an aquarium café).

The whole afternoon was sort of surreal. I mean, here was this boy I'd barely even said hello to before, and here we were right now, clicking so well, laughing so hard, relating on all sorts of levels.

And so completely attracted to one another.

It wasn't one of those love-at-first-sight kinds of attractions. Not like when, in the sixth grade, I saw the movie *The Sure Thing* with my best friend, Lisa DiLorenzo, and made a silent vow to myself—in the third row of the Loews Theatre, my mouth packed with popcorn and Jujyfruits—to one day meet and marry John Cusack.

*No*, it wasn't like that.

And, *no*, I never did carry through with that vow, though to this day there isn't a single Cusack film that makes it past my crush radar.

But I digress.

My conversation with Peter was easy, though—fluid, effortless—and at the same time it had a sort of where-have-you-been-all-my-life quality.

As cheesy as that sounds.

It was exactly how I felt.

There were moments in the conversation when Peter would look at me—really study me—and shake his head, as if somewhat taken aback. I was taken aback, too. I mean, why hadn't I ever noticed him before? Noticed what an amazing sense of humor he had, or how ice-blue his eyes were, or how his crooked smile had the power to turn my insides to mush?

"Since you're so fascinated with choices and consequences," he said after nearly three and a half hours of uninterrupted talk, "what do you think the consequence will be of us spending so much time together?"

I was hoping the answer was obvious. I mean, it was so completely clear to me that all signs were pointing to the best first date ever. But instead a girl appeared at our table, tearing a page out of what had otherwise been the start of a perfectly good love story.

Her hands placed firmly on her hips, she asked Peter where he'd been all this time. He looked at me as if I had the answer. But the only thing I knew for sure was that somehow I felt cheated.

And obviously so did she.

Peter ended up giving her a lame excuse—something about losing track of time and forgetting about their plans—and she stomped off, both angry and hurt.

I couldn't say that I blamed her.

"Shouldn't you go after her?" I asked him.

"Yeah," he said, "I definitely should." But his eyes remained fixed on mine, as if he didn't want to go just yet.

But finally he left, anyway.

The following day, after our writing class, we both lingered for a bit. The proverbial elephant in our now vacant classroom was who that girl was exactly, and why she'd been looking for him.

"My girlfriend and I were supposed to meet for lunch," he said, unable to even look at me now. "She'd been waiting for me at my apartment, and then had spent the next hour and a half hunting me down all over campus."

*His girlfriend.*

It's not that I hadn't expected it. It's just that a part of me had hoped there might have been some magical explanation.

"So then if you and your *girlfriend* had plans, what were you doing hanging out with me?" I asked him.

He bit his lip and met my eyes. "Why do you think?"

I looked away, wanting to hate him. But it was tough, especially when he told me how stupid he'd been, how bad he'd felt about the incident afterward, and how surprised he was that we'd clicked so well.

After that happened, I put up a wall—too high for even John Cusack to climb over. I forbade myself from gazing back at him in class, and I was forever one of the first people out the classroom door so as not to risk the possibility of talking to him. And getting myself involved.

It worked pretty well for a while, but then one afternoon toward the end of the semester, we found ourselves early for class. Peter was struggling to make small talk, asking me if I was ready for finals, and inquiring about the courses I'd be taking in the spring. Being a business major, I had room for only one humanities elective: Topics in Women's Studies with Professor Feener. I'd been looking forward to studying with her since first enrolling at the college.

That following semester, I remember walking into Feener's class on the first day and seeing Peter in the back row of a room full of females. I couldn't help but smile at how predictable—and yet unpredictable—he really was. I went and took the only empty seat beside him. And suddenly avoiding him was no longer a choice.

And my wall gave birth to a window.

During class lectures, we'd write notes back and forth in the margins of our notebooks, making fun of all sorts of silly stuff like how Professor Feener always clucked out her words, and how ironic it was that the girl sitting in front of us had anti-men stickers posted all over her peace-covered notebook.

Needless to say, things between us were really continuing to click, and I half expected for Peter to come to class one day and tell me that he and Morgan had broken up.

But nothing like that ever happened.

I'd see them together on campus—in the cafeteria, walking across the soccer field, and going off to the upperclassman apartments. I'd try to remind myself that things between us were innocent, and that I wasn't getting emotionally involved.

But I knew deep down that wasn't true.

Case in point: one day when Peter and I bumped into one another outside the library, I saw Morgan headed in our direction. And I bolted. Just like that. Because I didn't want her to "catch us."

The following day, Peter told me that Morgan was fine with he and I being friends, and that I had absolutely nothing to worry about.

So was I merely imagining things? Had I somehow misread the chemistry between us?

You tell me.

Suddenly Peter was appearing everywhere I was: in the café, in the parking lot by my car, waiting for me after class.

I wasn't the only one who noticed, either. People started asking if there wasn't something more going on between us. And then Peter told me about a dream he had—a dream in which he wanted more than anything to be with me, even though he knew he shouldn't.

"I can't even believe I just told you that," he said, standing by my car at the end of the night. The streetlamp illuminated a trace of stubble on his chin.

"Why *did* you tell me?" I asked.

"Because maybe I was kind of hoping you'd feel the same." His eyes drew a zigzag line down the center of my face, landing on my lips, causing my insides to rumble and stir.

"You have a girlfriend, Peter."

"I know."

"Then what?"

He shrugged and turned away, so I couldn't see his eyes— or maybe how truly vulnerable he looked.

"Do you love her?" I asked.

A simple enough question, but he didn't have an answer, and so he shrugged again and told me how great Morgan was— how unbelievably talented, and how she was his first real serious girlfriend.

"It's just that I never expected to meet someone like you," he said, running his fingers through his hair in frustration, as if meeting me was a bad thing.

And maybe it was.

Which is precisely the reason I decided to build up that wall again. I resisted the urge to respond to every amusing comment he scribbled into the margins of my notebook, and I did my best to appear busy or otherwise uninterested in what he had to say. But then Professor Feener paired us up to collaborate on a project.

And, once again, my wall came crumbling down.

I arranged to meet him at the library, hell-bent on keeping focused on our project, ironically the topic of which examined how the recurring theme of sexual desire in Kate Chopin's work is often suppressed by society's expectations, i.e., marriage and committed relationships. Suffice it to say, the discussion got a bit heated, especially when we turned to the topic of fate.

"What do you do when you're promised to someone, but then, by fate, you meet the person you're really supposed to be with?" he asked.

"I don't know," I told him. "What *do* you do?"

"What would *you* do?" he asked.

I shook my head, because I refused to tell him. Because I refused to be the one who would make or break his relationship. He'd have to do that on his own.

When the project was almost over, and the semester's end was near, we knew it'd be only a matter of weeks before graduation—before he'd move back home, clear across the country, and we'd probably never see each other again.

One night after a study session—when I should've headed off to my car, and he should've returned to his apartment—we found ourselves sitting on a nearby bench.

It was chilly outside, but the air was crisp. Overhead lights shined down over us, as did a waxing moon—both of which made me feel more exposed than I ever thought possible.

"So, what happens now?" he asked.

"What do you mean?" I said, completely aware that his question was fully loaded.

"I mean, how do you feel about me?"

A part of me wanted to tell him the truth—that I wished we could be together, that I found myself unable to stop and that I really did care about him.

I cared about him.

A lot.

"Well?" he asked when I didn't answer his question. He turned toward me again; his gray-blue eyes looked teary from the cold. "How *do* you feel about me?"

"I can't really say."

He swallowed hard; I watched the motion in his neck. "Why not?" he asked.

"Because you need to make your own decisions."

Peter's eyes wandered my face, perhaps wishing it'd reveal something, but I got up quickly before it could—before I'd cave and tell him everything.

While I strolled off in the moonlight by myself, he remained on the bench—deflated, tired and more disappointed than I'd ever seen him before.

But I was disappointed, too. Disappointed because he clearly wasn't the person that I wanted him to be.

The following day I heard the news that he and Morgan had gotten engaged the previous night. Apparently, sometime between blowing off their lunch date and asking me how I felt about him, he found the time to shop for a ring.

One of the last times I saw him, he said he'd like to meet up again at our five-year class reunion. I responded by telling him to have a nice life. Suffice it to say, I never did make it to the reunion—not just because of him; the truth is, I'm not exactly a reunion type person—but around year eight I got an email from him, asking me how I was and congratulating me on my writing career. He hinted about coming to my area on business. I told him that my life was very full, and then, once again, wished him well on his.

He's contacted me a few more times since then, but my wall remains permanently Peter proof. It's not that I have any hard feelings. It's just that once I made the decision to walk away from the situation—from someone who wasn't willing to put everything on the line to be with me—I never felt the need to look back.

A recent Google search tells me that he did indeed marry Morgan, and that they now have a family together. I'm happy for him, and I hope that he's happy. But still a part of me can't help but wonder what would've happened if he'd made a different decision back then, and if he's as pleased with the consequence as I am.*

* Please note that some of the names and minor details have been altered to protect the now-married-with-children. My married-with-children, on the other hand, knows all about this story, and loves me more for it.

# Crush Me

## Suzanne Finnamore

In its most literal interpretation, to *crush* (squash/squeeze/mash/pound/devastate) is to be forced into a compressed position, a position of submission to a greater power. In its context as a romantic state, the literal meaning of *crush* has not, to my mind, been sufficiently remarked upon. I intend to clarify this in as explicit a manner as I can manage, hopefully without becoming impossibly strident, diffident or bitter. However, I make no promises. If you are a romantic and sentimental sort of person expecting gossamer prose that makes you well up with tears and dash off to scribe meaningful and warm phrases in your journal, I suggest you cease reading this and move on to the fictional works of Danielle Steel, Nicholas Sparks or Robert James Waller.

If your quest is for unfettered sentiment, in particular, Robert James Waller pours rapt, boundless energy into all that capers and wafts down a rose-petal path; he will not cause you a moment's doubt in the Heart's Desire and Soul Mate aisle, replete with claw-foot bathtubs and handwritten notes pinned on quaint covered bridges in the slanting evening sun. In exchange for a tale of the killer crush, Waller will give you that marvelous oxymoron: a Good Cry. I freely admit he gave one to me.

*The Bridges of Madison County* was a runaway bestseller, instantly made into a blockbuster film with Meryl Streep and Clint Eastwood (although no one I knew claimed to have read a single page or seen the movie; what notorious liars people are). Watch the movie. It's impossibly wrenching and poignant, even though one suspects that in the modern world, our barefoot heroine, Francesca the Farmwife with Italian Sex Appeal, would have paired off with her paramour, Robert Kincaid the Dashing Photographer/Cowboy with an Excellent Position at *National Geographic*. Francesca would have, one intuits, procured a nice sensible divorce, and probably kept a few acres of the farm in the bargain. Custodial trips to Venice and the Uffizi would have ensued, offspring enjoying summer months at a villa in Tuscany (still affordable in the sixties). Everyone would have worked things out for the sake of the children. Farmer husband would have understood, grateful for the time he had managed to have with Francesca, who was wistful to the point of suicide for most of their marriage. Farmer husband would have remarried a local girl, and in time the humiliation would have been borne. You know it would have.

Yet the film, set in 1962, holds the Family Value line, rejecting the idea that Robert Kincaid and Francesca's extreme crush, their four-day breakneck love affair, could see them safely through the rest of their lives; it shuns the sudden and potent crush of impromptu love as a serious contender. Very convincing it is:

during the climactic Great Sacrifice scene, when Francesca almost but not quite flings open the passenger's side door of her husband's pickup truck to run toward her lover, I nearly collapsed a lung weeping. The red light that Francesca and her farmer husband are stopped at, just behind Eastwood's truck, goes on being red for what seems like a full eternity while Francesca kneads, rubs and grapples the door handle; she almost pulls it out of the goddamned car door. (Eastwood, who, earlier, was standing in the rain, looking bereft as a clubbed baby seal, straddles a very fine line between masterfully tender and puerile.) But it is 1962, and so I notice Francesca does not get out of her warm, dry vehicle. I notice she understands that what she and the flinty-eyed, roving *National Geographic* photographer have is not a serious love, but rather a crush...one that might crush her and her entire family if she got out of that rickety-ass truck—she suspects that if she had played it through, her crush on Kincaid might flourish, throw out seed and inadvertently choke her bucolic life's well-tended, deeply rooted garden.

As if to confirm its lack of seriousness, the word *crush* in a romantic sense is not recognized in traditional dictionaries—in their expert opinion it is an ethereal thing and cannot be pinned down to a fact or definition. So I turned to the Urban Dictionary, which traffics heavily in cultural catchphrases and ineffable matter of all kinds.

In the Urban Dictionary, the second definition of *crush* is "a painful experience, very common among middle schoolers (and high schoolers and even adults to a lesser degree) that involves being obsessed with a member of the opposite sex (or the same sex, if you prefer), being attracted to them physically (most common), or emotionally—also called 'puppy love'."

At the ripe age of eight, had I known what a *crush* was when it entered my bloodstream—and blood it was, make no mistake—I might have opted for a more supine position in the general scheme of things. Instead I ran to embrace it like a trusted ally. I thought, *Well, this is a good feeling, what a glory, what a marvelous sensation, tingling and engulfing body and mind. I intend to please the object of my crush as hard and as convincingly as I can, even if it means giving up a few afternoons of going to the library, jettisoning girlfriends, disobeying my parents and teachers, keeping dangerous secrets or giving up my own soul. And if I am very, very lucky, I will be crushed back. Oh, yes, what a glory, what a marvelous sensation, is traversing my body to the ends of my hair. I have no thought for anything except this very moment, and perhaps the one after.*

To be in the moment may very well be the best thing the average crush has to recommend for it. Let us not confuse it with love. It doesn't want love's duties, its complexities. It is the soft drink of emotions.

To confirm my point, I see where in its fourth definition, the Urban Dictionary defines *crush* as: "a kick-ass bottled soda pop made in orange, grape, and strawberry flavors. Comes in six-packs. Example: *I drank nine bottles of Crush today.*"

Soft, perhaps, but with undeniable merits: certainly it has pleasure going for it, and some importance; a cold soft drink can be delicious and even lifesaving, if one is in the desert without the benefit of a canteen.

Then again, there are nefarious, darker meanings to *crush*—see definition six in the Urban Dictionary: "Verb. The process by which people are killed when thrown beneath a steamroller or placed in between two solid surfaces with force being applied toward them that the body cannot withstand."

Historically there is the witch *crush:* the medieval process of laying one flagstone upon another and another, until the alleged sorceress's body trapped beneath the stones is unable to draw breath, her bones broken like so much peanut brittle—often performed to the recitation of religious passages, and with many capering, excited onlookers—with the end result of pressing alleged witches into the ground until they are dead. This reinforces my feeling that *crush* and *crushing* may not be the harmless, gay concepts they parade as.

Much later, sometime around the 1990s, *crush* in the sense of being infatuated became a verb; in the same way many nouns that had no business being animated became verbs. *Network* became a verb, and this was vastly troubling. And *crush* became a verb, the better to toss from here to there. Grown people took on the term… and in so doing, it was ruined for children and teenagers, in the same way that Facebook was ruined for them when their parents usurped it.

Yes, I do stray from the original point of this essay. Perhaps I dance and flit around the subject because I am overwhelmed by the (greedy, fleeting and petulant) conviction that all crushes and giddy emotions have passed me by, like an express train headed for a fine metropolitan center, while I—awash in children, stepchildren and the quotidian of being past twelve, in a time when our economy and our country are anything but buoyant and youthful—stand at the doorway of my home, holding a frying pan and a spatula with which to pry the daily egg.

Disclaimer: Let me explain my outlook on the crush, in the present moment. This week in my shared household with my fiancé, Tom, forty-nine, we are horribly short on time and adequate child care or slow dancing; our ratio of children to adults is sixteen thousand to one. And so the eggs and cooking utensils and laundry loads of my life as an engaged, divorced mother have become overwhelming. The relentless homework and crying toddlers and mac-and-cheese-encrusted meals of my life have taken seniority over the niceties of bubbling feelings. Therefore I am hard-pressed to feel the proper ebullient outlook toward crushes and a gay, insouciant state of being.... The right tone has not been set. I admit this.

But let the record state that despite all, I absolutely do want to *crush* on a regular basis, to—like Francesca and Robert Kincaid—have my hair washed by my beloved and make love for hours at a time while a big band station plays on an old radio and brandy in thin snifters is imbibed at a Formica table, all children tucked away at a 4-H meeting in Kansas with a responsible farmer. I want to continuously *crush*. Although, it must be noted, Tom and I sharing a massive crush and parlaying it into love and commitment and a blended family is absolutely what led me to this very position in the doorway, with the spatula and the frying pan. I don't see how it could have been avoided, as we both came into the relationship with past crushes and so forth under our belts; we entered this undertaking as adults with several children, some of them small.

Why don't I just say it: *Crushes lead to love lead to marriage lead to children, which lead to the grave.* Yes. Here, I—quite waspish, racked with fatigue, and without the proper perspective—state this without the frill of political correctness or the maternal yoke of everlasting gratitude, grace and feminine forbearance around my neck.

In my defense, I look to self-honesty and truth telling as a pressure release valve, so that within this venue I may consider the topic of the sweet, deep, uncomplicated *crush* without being blasé and preemptive. In fact, I would posit that this essay's (rather horrify-

ing, I admit) honest and confessional tone is a kind of *inner crush*...
a *crush* on myself, on my past and perhaps the child-free future, a
*crush* on my own freedom. To consider the time when I was a girl
and could dally in infatuation, the time I could, with no thought of
consequence or Right or Wrongdoing, indulge a flood of sensual
feeling, release the emotion love dogs willy-nilly. The time I could
walk home at a leisurely pace, at age eight, with thoughts of Jimmy
Duke and his way of riding his Stingray bike with real abandon.

Jimmy Duke was my first *crush*. I meant to say this in
the beginning, but other things took over. On the school yard of
Allendale Elementary in Oakland, California, on a short fifty-yard
asphalt race course painted with five white lanes Jimmy Duke
and I raced, just the two of us, while Roy Campbell looked on in
mild interest on his Schwinn bike with the playing cards stuck in
the spokes. Jimmy Duke won, although I tried my fierce best and
almost lost a shoe. He won and he said nothing, because for Jimmy
Duke, winning was a given. (This says it all, crush-wise. In my time,
most women—even girls on the brink of becoming women—want
men who win and say nothing. We do not want to triumph over
men in any physical way; it is not sexy and it goes against the bio-
logical imperatives that keep human beings from being wiped off
the earth by insects and crabgrass.)

Jimmy Duke had a crooked smile, the flaw being the very
entry point of the *crush* knife. Historically, I have always spent
my crushes on males with elemental good looks but an array of
interesting flaws that distinguish them from the other, more perfect and some would say pretty boys, the plethora of narcissistic
men-children that grow thick on the ground in California—especially San Francisco, Marin County, San Diego and the greater
Los Angeles area.

Jimmy's hair was sandy and straight, with body. A boy with body in his straight hair is not to be trifled with; he has an advantage over the stingy-haired boys who are constantly peering out from a curtain of hair. Curtains of hair are a plus for girls, but for boys, a curtain of hair is a liability. It suggests femininity and perhaps a lack of stiffness, a bit less confidence, which may in fact lead to impotence in his later years. (No one wants to admit it, but a mostly reliable and stiff penis is sometimes all that stands between a successful union and a lackluster and grim union of potentially obese individuals. Without sex, heterosexual men and women would never have anything to do with one another beyond procreation, the impromptu rearrangement of furniture and.... Well, I can't think of another activity they might share willingly and with a benefit to anyone.)

Roy Campbell had a Moe Howard hairstyle and Roy Campbell hung around Jimmy Duke, looking to scoop up his leftover girls. This worked well until Roy Campbell developed acute acne and was summarily shunned by girls of all ages. Later, he developed a fondness for controlled substances. So that's it. My first crush, accompanied by his wingman.

Fast-forward to the present. My own fiancé, Tom, has hair that sticks straight up and don't I know it. It stands at attention and is ready for what happens next. It never falls into his eyes or threatens to conceal or flop on his face in ways that could only mean a weakness in character.

Tom is unquestionably the biggest *crush* of my life, arriving—to my chagrin—after I had already married and divorced and given up on anything like crushes, secretly feeling that love, perhaps, was "an affliction curable by marriage," to crib from Ambrose Bierce.

So it is lovely that the Urban Dictionary nails and also validates my at-first-sight *crush* on Tom, in its definition number three:

1. The act of falling hard for someone even though it isn't love yet
2. A precursor to love
3. An amazing thing that gives you feelings of nerves and excitement whenever you see them

Since the day we met, I seem to have been stripped of all knowledge save emotional and carnal knowledge. (Surely the way this essay meanders is proof positive of this theory.) In my "nerves and excitement," I am very close to being a mildly retarded adult, happy almost 100 percent of the time. The difference is that I am happy approximately 80 percent of the time; the rest of the time I am fearful and anxious that my happiness will be snatched from me.

But Tom is very close to being an evolved and perfect mate for me. This is why I have agreed to marry him, despite my suspicion that all crushes are doomed, and that marriage is a conspiracy from Tiffany's, the diamond industry and the Christian Fundamentalists. Whenever I try to sabotage our union, or wax jaded and pessimistic about our love, Tom deftly and summarily quashes my dissent in firm and absolute terms. He will not brook dissent in the ranks; like many fine and good German Americans he has his fascistic, impeccable standards and they will not be chipped at. He is the most Teutonic man I have ever known, unassailable and zealous in his ability to work, to be perennially practical and patient, and take me in hand when I run amok and begin to be crazy, which is my default setting. Having fallen for the greatest and most solid love of my life, I am fully and with emphasis carried away from my shabby notion of independence and intellectual distinction.

Tom, while performing his full-time job and caring for his children and my own, is also taking on infatuation side effects; he is exhibiting brain damaged characteristics. For example, yesterday he ran full force into a seven-foot metal pole in his backyard, in broad daylight and while under the influence of this deceptively innocuous thing, the *crush*. He is being crushed under the wheels of infatuation that became infected with love and is, at this very moment, headed toward the gully of Marriage, where much will be lost but much will be gained. We will be wed. What will become of us?

Whatever happens, the ubiquitous *crush* was the genesis of—to quote from *Zorba the Greek*—"the full catastrophe." Let us lobby for it to have its own place in *Webster's*, if not a sacred nook in our lives. Amen.

# Love, Illustrated

## Melissa Walker

On the first day of ninth grade, I carry an extra notebook with me. It isn't for science or math or English or history. It's for writing down my thoughts as I go through this new experience—because I want to be a writer, and my dad says I need to observe the world in order to make that happen. So the notebook is a plain red spiral model, with pages white as daisy petals, ready for my brilliant ruminations.

I'm walking out of the end-of-alphabet homeroom, in which I have no friends. (Why, as a *W* girl, are my best friends Lindsay Adams and Jessica Becker? We will never be alphabetically connected.) And just as I turn the corner toward my first class, schedule in hand, there he is: Matt Garner. He's more muscular than I remember from seventy-two days ago, when I last saw him on the final afternoon of eighth grade, and he's tan from the summer sun. His family belongs to the country club. He lives in The Dogwoods, a rich neighborhood, and his older brother is a senior, so he doesn't have to ride the bus. He even made varsity football this year—as a *freshman*. His life is charmed.

You may think this is going to be one of those moments where the shy girl walks by and doesn't say anything to her popular-guy crush. But here's what you don't know about Matt Garner: He's nice. And he likes me. I mean, he doesn't *like* like me, that I know of, but he does appreciate me as a person. He thinks I'm smart and funny, and he used to talk to me a lot in earth science last year. He always signs my yearbook really thoughtfully, which is something that I—as a word geek—notice and value more than the average fourteen-year-old.

He's fidgeting with the handle of his locker, frowning and looking like he's having trouble, but then he turns. He sees me. He smiles. "Hey, Melissa," he says. I mean, he uses my name and he flashes that grin and my heart speeds up. This is official acknowledgment. And in the hallway, in public! I can feel my cheeks start to warm as I cluck out a "Hello." This is the thing about Matt: He isn't party to the normal social grouping rules. He talks to everyone. He knows their names. He laughs easily. People flock to him.

If I were remotely socially skilled, I would start up a conversation. "How was your summer?" is on the tip of my tongue, but it feels so generic, so bland. So I opt for nothing, which is even lamer.

I try not to get distracted by his gigantic blue eyes or his wavy brown hair, and I fix my gaze on the number of the locker he's been struggling to open: 286. I pull out a pen and scribble the digits onto the corner of my new red notebook. Then I keep walking down the hall.

And that's how it starts: Notebook 286, also known as the book of Stalking Matt Garner. Of course, I don't think of what I'm doing as stalking. I tell myself that it's more watching, observing. You know, as a way to build my writing career.

Over the next week, I write an entire fantasy sequence in my Notebook 286, one where Matt Garner takes me in his arms on that first day of school and dances me through the hallways, making everyone jealous as we twirl and twirl to the Cure's "Just Like Heaven," which is somehow being pumped through the school speakers.

I even write dialogue, including "This summer was empty without you" (that's his line) and "I've always thought you were quietly beautiful" (also him). I don't write much dialogue for myself, actually. I prefer my fantasy self to smile coyly and accept Matt's lavish attention.

I keep the notebook by my side in order to record any interactions with Matt Garner, however slight. Each day, I write down every single word Matt says to me. And sometimes I draw some stick figures with word bubbles, just to make the pages less sparse. In between the real-life pages, I've started my own sort of reality-fantasy novel. There's a little voice in the back of my head that says that's kind of sad, but I ignore it.

During week two of the new year, though, I get careless with Notebook 286. Lindsay sees it.

"What are you drawing?" she asks, leaning over my shoulder at lunch. We're sitting outside on the quad, at a perfect angle to watch Matt and the other football guys, who are taking over a large picnic table.

As Lindsay reaches for Notebook 286, I'm doodling the football picnic table on the first page.

I tighten my grip on Notebook 286 and pull it into my chest.

Thankfully something distracts Lindsay.

"What's Amy Mason doing at the football table?" asks Lindsay, looking off in Matt's direction.

My head whips around. Amy's got her hand on Matt's shoulder.

"And why's her hair all blond?" asks Jessica, slurring her words a little as she licks the top of her yogurt container.

"Summer makeover," I whisper, in awe of what I'm seeing.

As Amy throws her long, way-more-blond-than-last-May hair over her shoulder, I see that her chest size has amped up even more than her highlights. She is stacked. The braces? Gone. The thick glasses? Missing.

"Contacts and dental work," says Lindsay knowingly. "Not to mention a major boob spurt."

I can't believe it. I guess I thought this kind of over-the-summer change happened only in movies—not in real life on the quad in front of my eyes. But there it is: Amy Mason is a babe. And judging by the way they're looking at each other, she's also with Matt Garner.

By the end of the week, it's confirmed. Amy and Matt spent time together playing tennis at the country club over the summer, and they've been dating since the week before school started. Matt dating Amy Mason hurts more than if he were dating Callie Leive or Jenny Banks or even Tory Geist—because those girls have always been popular. They're part of his crowd.

But Amy Mason? Last year she was...well, she was like me.

I spend a few minutes one morning staring in the mirror. The boob thing is out of my control, but I'm half wishing I had thick glasses and crooked teeth that I could fix so I'd make a Hollywood-esque transformation at school. But what I have is just a bunch of average parts that add up to a wholly pedestrian package. I'm ordinary. I'm like the person you'd cast as an extra in a party scene so that the pretty people would shine but there wouldn't be someone crazily ugly in the background, just some plain people without their own style.

I lace up my Converse—the one semi-fashionable clothing item I own—and grab Notebook 286. Despite the Amy Mason development, the pages are filling up. I refuse to put her bubble boobs into the stories I'm writing. My most recent one involves Matt asking me to the Thanksgiving Dance, which is actually a girls-ask-boys thing, but I imagine he's so in love with me that he has to take charge. I even describe the outfit I'd wear: classy black silk strapless dress with a bubble skirt. I read in a magazine that when you wear black silk, you can pull off a playful silhouette. I draw a picture of my outfit, but it looks more like a kid's cartoon than a fashion sketch.

As my Me-and-Matt-Garner fantasy world grows in Notebook 286, the pages that catalog our real-life interactions are fewer and farther between. We don't have any classes together, which is killing me, but Matt and I do pass each other in the halls twice a day, between second and third periods, and between sixth and seventh periods. On a good day, Matt will actually say, "Hey, Melissa," and I write that down, usually surrounded by a heart doodle or squiggly, excited lines. On an average afternoon, he'll smile and nod at me, no vocal acknowledgment. And on a bad day, he won't see me. I'm always looking for him, and I know the exact moment when we usually pass—right before I get to the water fountain at the end of the math hall.

I've taken to bringing Notebook 286 with me everywhere, even outside of school, as if the very fact of my carrying it gives me a better shot at seeing Matt around town. One Saturday, Lindsay and I are waiting for my mom to pick us up after an afternoon movie, and there he is. Matt's sitting on the bench outside the theater exit, and he looks like he's waiting, too.

When I walk onto the street, I see him immediately, but Lindsay's talking about how much she liked the movie we just saw, so she keeps babbling and I'm grateful not to have to stand there awkwardly. I laugh, too loudly, at what Lindsay's saying. I feel the need to exaggerate my glee in front of Matt Garner. It's like I'm onstage and I need to wear too much makeup and talk extra loud so the audience gets it.

*Do you get it, Matt Garner?* My best friend and I are here, we're hilarious, and I am very social on this Saturday afternoon at the movies. Look at me! I'm delightful! I don't even notice you! I'm so happy and fun!

"Melissa?" Matt stands up from his bench and comes over to us. Heart pounding, mind recording every movement and precious word, I instinctively put my hand on the canvas tote bag at my side, patting Notebook 286 with the knowledge that today will get a special weekend entry.

Our interaction ends up being little more than "What movie did you see?" before my mom's Pontiac rolls up to the curb and interrupts us. I wave to Matt and take a mental picture of him waving back, and I can hardly wait to drop Lindsay off so I can get home and open the notebook.

In my rendition of this afternoon's interaction, I change some "factual" details: 1) I'm wearing a skirt in the picture, when in reality, I'm wearing the same pair of jeans I always wear; 2) In the comic I draw, I make the last frame a little wistful by drawing Matt's mouth as a squiggly line, like he's sad my mom interrupted us; 3) In the notebook's depiction, Lindsay isn't there.

You have to understand that in Notebook 286, only two people exist. It's just me and Matt, stick figures in love, on those pages. No one can interrupt our uncomplicated little 2-D world.

Then one day the school bus I normally take breaks down; we have to borrow the football team's away-game bus. I don't mind this turn of events—I'll probably even draw a cartoon in Notebook 286 about riding Matt's bus. Even though he's not on it.

As I ease onto a brown vinyl seat near the back, I notice a paper triangle in the space between the seat cushion and the wall of the bus. It's one of those folded-up loose-leaf footballs that guys play with at lunch in a game I've never quite understood.

I fish it out of the crack and run my fingers along the triangle's smooth edges—it's carefully made, I notice, as I inspect it more closely. Then I see that there's something written inside the folds... in all capital letters.

*Matt writes in all caps,* I think as I slowly pull apart the paper football. And now I can see that it's a real note—a long one. It fills one side of a whole page, and it starts with "Amy..." I glance around to see if anyone else has seen me with this note that isn't mine, but that belongs to my one true love, or maybe his girlfriend. No one's looking.

I pause before I read it. It seems impossible that this note could have fallen in my lap, like an unbelievable plot twist in a silly romantic comedy. But here it is. I take a deep breath.

The note says a lot of things. It compares Amy to a shooting star, and also references a really bad Michael J. Fox movie called *Doc Hollywood.* It's clear that Matt is pouring his heart out. I don't discover anything really juicy, unless you count the fact that Matt is head over heels for Amy as really juicy. He loves her, it seems.

I trudge home slowly, wondering what I'll write in Notebook 286 today. Maybe nothing. I know I shouldn't keep the note— it's not for me—but I'm not sure how to dispose of it. I consider throwing it away, but I can't. Matt did write it, after all, even if he didn't write it for me.

In the privacy of my bedroom, I use a glue stick to adhere the note to a page of Notebook 286. It's a masochistic move, but I want to keep it.

After reading Amy's note for a fifth time, I decide to flip back through the pages of Notebook 286 to enjoy some of my interactions with Matt. Aren't I special to him, too?

As I read my chronicles, though, it's clear that the answer is no. At least, I'm not special like Amy is special. All I'm reading is a long list of "Hey, Melissa"s and "Nod"s and "He didn't see me"s. And I realize, now that I have a real note that shows how expressive Matt can be, that Notebook 286 might as well be subtitled "A Chronicle of Patheticness."

I feel a lump in my throat as I close the red cover. It's not a recording of my romantic history, not a love poem, not a great art project. It's the scribbles of a girl in love with a boy who doesn't know and doesn't care.

I don't take Notebook 286 to school the next day. It sits under my bed, catching dust bunnies on its rounded corners.

The fall of freshman year continues, Matt and Amy keep dating, and I try to find other guys to like. I start adding new drawings to Notebook 286.

In the spring, I look through the Matt Garner pages of Notebook 286 again. *Okay, the reality part is a little hard to read, but the fantasy scenes are actually well done,* I think. Maybe this crush's purpose was to inspire me to dream up dramatic and heart-soaring love scenes. Maybe noticing the tiniest details about Matt Garner was an exercise in observation that will help me down the line. Maybe I can be a writer, after all. As it turns out, I did become a writer, mining these very angsty moments for my teen novels and giving the main characters some of my own insecurities (while the lead guys get some of Matt's sparkle and charm).

Of course, I had real relationships of the three-dimensional kind as time went on.

My first boyfriend came around during my senior year of high school, and he absolutely adored me. He made me laugh so hard I'd snort. In college, my two relationships included one guy who wrote letters and made mix tapes, and another who whisked me off for weekend vacations away from campus. After graduation, out in the real world, I had a steady stream of boyfriends who brought me flowers, told me I was beautiful, showed up for me at a moment's notice when I told them I needed them. And now? I'm married to a guy who doesn't let a day go by without telling me how much he loves me, and why.

I'm not saying Matt Garner gets credit for my string of exceedingly excellent guys. After all, I found them. I'm just saying that Matt Garner gave me more than good material for my young adult novels. He was the perfect first big crush because he was kind, generous and friendly. Even though we never dated, he treated me with such friendship that I learned to expect that from guys I liked. I never once went after the bad boy.

Matt married a good friend of mine, in the end. I went to their wedding and felt not a pang of jealousy. And when they came to my wedding last summer that great guy I married let go of me so that I could take a spin across the dance floor with Matt Garner.*

---

* *Names of friends and crushes have been changed because this episode of my life is totally embarrassing and I don't want to humiliate them by association.*

# What We Know Now

## Katie Herzog

Until I was twenty years old, my twin sister was the most important person in my life. We spent nine months floating together and grew up in tandem, half a pair rather than a person alone. My sister and I are fraternal twins, no more genetically similar than any siblings. We are, in fact, very different. She's five-five; I'm five-six. She has straight hair; I have curly hair. She has a master's degree; I was kicked out of high school for building a papier-mâché bong in art class. In a twenty-year-old video that our father made, the camera so large it rests on his shoulder, my sister and I stand in front of our childhood home in matching Easter dresses. She beams at the camera with missing front teeth and a basket full of pastel eggs. I scowl and kick a rotting stump, unhappy about the pink lace and puffy sleeves our mother made us wear. My sister wears white socks and patent leather shoes. I'm in snow boots and a baseball cap. But despite the differences, we came into the world together, and so, for the first twenty years of our lives, we loved each other more than anyone else.

But then, on my twentieth birthday, I met Alice. Though I had never been with a woman, I had long been attracted to them, and so I wasn't shocked that when I saw Alice at my birthday party, it felt electric. At the time, I lived in a dirty co-op beside a halfway house. When we threw parties—kegs in the backyard, underage kids on the porch—the men who lived next door watched us through their windows. They would have seen Alice and me kissing against a wall that night, drunk and dizzy and half-aware that everything was changing.

Soon, we were the couple that ignores friends and family and lives in a bubble for two. When I woke up in the morning and walked to the kitchen to start coffee and pour cereal, Alice would prance in a few minutes later, curls perched atop her head so she looked like the love child of Lyle Lovett and a T. rex. She would jump around in her underwear, waking us both up, growling like a bear. It was impossible to wake up in a bad mood when I was with her.

Still, I was terrified that Alice would realize I wasn't good enough for her, that she would stop calling and coming over and touching my foot with hers in her sleep. I concocted wild schemes to make her fall in love with me. *If only she could see how precious I am when I'm sleeping,* I thought; and so, more than once, I ran to my bed when she was coming over and pretended to nap, my eyelids fluttering quietly, my mouth open just so. Alice thought I was lazy, not darling, but still, we fell in love. I was so in love with Alice that I sometimes wondered if I had to choose between my girlfriend and my sister, who I would choose, and then felt sorry for my sister.

More than making Alice happy, I wanted to make her safe. My reason was selfish: I would stop breathing if she did. I started dreaming about natural disasters. I became paranoid about earthquakes and floods. I stocked up on canned goods and jugs of water. Over dinner, I made my Alice recite our plan in case of the Second Coming and later bought us matching walkie-talkies, insisting that this simple technology would be our salvation when the cell towers collapsed. I didn't know then that it wouldn't be a natural disaster that would split us up; it would be something innocuous and everywhere.

Alice and I went through the coming-out process together. My friends and my sister were unfazed when I told them I was dating a woman. As a kid, I was the only girl in Little League. People addressed me as "young man" so often that I started answering to it without a thought. No one was surprised that I was gay, but still, I didn't want to come out to my parents.

When people come out of the closet, our parents often say things like, "It's not that I hate gay people. I just don't want your life to be more difficult than your brother's. He might be in prison, but at least he can get married." This was not my fear. My parents raised us with only a cursory awareness of religion. If not for the prevalence of religion in our Southern hometown—warnings of eternal damnation broadcast from billboards with statements like, "What if Jesus had been aborted?"—I suspect I would have started college wondering why so many people wear Ts around their necks. So the problem was not that I was afraid my parents would be disappointed. I didn't want to tell them, because telling your parents you're gay means telling them that you aren't just emotionally and mentally gay. You're gay in bed. It is terrible enough to think about your parents' sex life; think about how much worse it is for them. I was their little girl. I sat on their laps and giggled when they tickled me and cried when they spanked me for starting a small and completely manageable fire in the neighbor's yard.

But it was inevitable. A few months after Alice and I got together, my sister called. "Mom knows you're gay," she said. Despite my fear of rebuke, my parents were more worried about my lapsed health insurance than my sexual orientation. When I asked my mother who told her, she said, "No one. Your father has gaydar." It was a fine coming-out, easy, something I should have done long before. But when Alice came out, her mother cried and her dad said it was just a phase. He was wrong. It wasn't a phase, and two years later, we moved across the country together.

If my first love was innate and my second consuming, my third was both. I had always been a drinker, but it was after Alice and I moved that I became as enamored with drinking as I was with her. I loved the way liquor warmed, beer cooled, and wine flushed my cheeks. I hid my drinking from Alice. I drank on our back porch when she was asleep and during the day, when she was at work. I went to bars and parties when she was too tired to attend. And I cheated. Again and again, I made out with strangers at bars and at parties and even, more than once, went back to their houses for terrible, drunken sex. I slept with people I liked and people I hated. I wanted them all for the newness, the possibility that I would feel electric, like I had on my twentieth birthday. I never did.

Alice didn't know about the others, but still, we started to fight, and loudly. Our neighbors looked at us strangely when we ran into them in the mail room. After Alice punched a wall and sprained her elbow after a particularly vicious fight, probably about something unimportant, I went to a bar up the street. The bartender was going through his own breakup at the time and poured deep glasses of bourbon for both of us. A few hours later, I passed out on the bathroom floor, slumped against the wall. Alice had been wandering the neighborhood, trying to find me, and when she did, she hauled me outside and into the rain. I lay on the sidewalk in front of the bar. She kicked me in the kidneys and yelled that I was a drunk and a whore, and then she hailed a cab, got me in the house and left me to sleep it off on the bathroom floor.

The next day, I received a call from my sister across the country. When she checked her voice mail that morning, she had heard a long and muffled fight as Alice tried to get me off the sidewalk and into the cab. "There are things," she said, "I just don't want to hear."

But because Alice and I loved each other as much as we hated each other, she forgave me for passing out at the bar, I forgave her for kicking me in the back, and we laughed about pocket dialing my sister.

Two weeks later, Alice found out about my cheating when she read an email I had sent to my sister asking for advice. As soon as she found out, Alice drove to the bakery where I had just started working. I saw her face, red and violent, from my place behind the register. Without a word, she pulled her fist back and let it go from across the counter—one right hook to the jaw and the collective gasp of a dozen onlookers.

I ended the day both homeless and jobless. I slept on a friend's couch for a few days and then I called my sister across the country and asked her to pick me up at the airport the next day. I didn't say goodbye to anyone.

I kept drinking when I moved away. The more I drank, the more my life became a series of misadventures.

I went out every night. I met girls at bars and parties, held their hands as we walked back to my house, promising to make breakfast in the morning. The next day, I always pretended to be asleep until they left. After these nights, I told the stories to my friends. They laughed and shook their heads, amused and unsurprised that I had sex in a bar bathroom with someone whose name I couldn't quite remember but was pretty sure started with a *J.* But every time I woke up beside a new woman, I paused for a moment before opening my eyes, wishing for just a second that the woman beside me wasn't the one I met at the bar last night; wishing it to be her, to be Alice, returned from the past and ready to forgive. I kept drinking.

Late one night, alone at my house, I smoked a cigarette on my porch and tossed it close to but not into the ashtray. I then went inside to watch *Rescue Me,* a television show about the New York City Fire Department, which is full of drunks and heroes. When it was over, I got off my couch and took another beer from my fridge and walked to my porch. When I opened the door, I saw fire climbing the wall beside my empty ashtray.

I threw my beer onto the fire, and when that didn't work, I grabbed the fire extinguisher and sprayed the wall and thought about how I would have to clean the remnants tomorrow. When the fire extinguisher was empty, the embers were still burning in the wall. I called 911 and told the dispatcher that I didn't want to tell him my name and address, because I didn't want to get in trouble, but he was insistent and soon the fire trucks were screaming in my driveway. Before I ran outside, I grabbed the flask of vodka I kept in my freezer and hid it in my pocket. When the firemen arrived, I noted that their boots were getting dirt on my floor and I'd have to clean that, too. They dragged the hose upstairs and across my newly vacuumed carpet and asked me what started the fire. "Spontaneous combustion," I said. This did not make them laugh or even smile. I told the fire chief that it couldn't have been a cigarette, that I don't smoke because it's disgusting, and besides, even if I did, it's a nonsmoking building.

After the fire was out—planks missing from my porch, siding and installation charred, everything covered in ash—and the firefighters rolled up their hose, they shook my hand and congratulated me for not panicking, for using the fire extinguisher, for calling 911. It seemed ridiculous to shake my hand after I'd started a fire, and I said this, but, no, they said, "If you hadn't acted then, the fire would have spread to the roof."

I finished the rest of the vodka and tried to sleep but my sheets smelled like campfire and my head was spinning so much that I had to keep one foot on the floor. I thought about my neighbors, about the guy next door who lives with his sister and has a thousand dollars' worth of miniature cars. I thought about the neighbors on the other side with a wicker pentagram on their front door and the neighbor downstairs who thinks I'm a boy, and I thought about the neighbors a few units down who had just gotten engaged and had this whole new part of their lives happening. Three more minutes, the firemen said, and the fire would have slid across the roof and taken the Hot Wheels and the wedding invitations and we would be people who lost things in a fire.

My sister came over the next day, furious, not just that I started a fire, but that I was drinking alone on a Tuesday night. She yelled at me through angry tears, screaming that I could have killed myself or someone else. She was tired, she said, of worrying if I was going to spend the night at home or in the hospital or in jail. My problems had become Alice's problems and now my problems were becoming my sister's problems and this couldn't happen again. It was time, finally, to break up with booze.

Over the next few weeks, I mopped my kitchen floor and cleaned my fridge and contributed to the NPR fund drive. I got a library card and running shoes and planted tomatoes in my yard. Staying sober was hardest right before dark, when my friends were at their usual spots at the bar, lifting bottles and telling stories. When the itch started, all I wanted was a night of complete oblivion, when you achieve an almost Buddhist state, when there is no yesterday and no tomorrow and no consequence as long as the bottle is in your hand. I probably would have given up at the first itch, but there was my sister, watching. I listened to her problems instead of talking about mine. She told me about work, about her ex-boyfriends, about her life. I listened, and after a few weeks, when the parkinsonian tremor retreated and my brain was no longer muddy, I looked at the tomatoes growing outside of my window and was happy.

Will it last forever? Will I never again wake up in an emergency room or a stranger's bed? Maybe. But gin in the summer and bourbon in the winter are so good, and so, too, is the possibility of relapse, of knowing that even if I ruin everything, even if Alice and my sister and all the rest are gone, my third love will always have me back.

But for now, it's just my sister and me, like it was in the beginning. She's five-five; I'm five-six. She's in patent leather shoes; I'm in snow boots. She thinks of men and wishes there was just one good one to call her own. And I think of her, of Alice, of this stupid, sad exile from the one who loved me violently, the one I can't forget.

# Just a Friend

## Brendan Halpin

I like you as a friend.

Almost all my teen crushes ended with me hearing these words. No, sadly, that's actually not true. Most of them continued even after those cruel words. Because, I thought, if she likes me as a friend, can liking me as a boyfriend be far behind?

Yes. Yes, it can. It can be very, very far behind.

But I had a really spectacular ability to delude myself, and so I was convinced that all they needed in order to see the error of their ways was more time in my company to appreciate my brilliance and rapier wit. And then they'd want to kiss me!

Sadly, it never once occurred to me that I should, for example, take better care of my appearance, that "clean, but otherwise un-kempt" is not really a look that inspires the ladies to swoon with desire, at least not in the teenage years. No, in my teen mind, the problem was with these foolish girls who preferred a good-looking athlete to a slightly doughy, incredibly sarcastic genius with tragically bad hair.

And so, when I look back now at most of my teen crushes, I feel dumb, either because I wasted time liking the wrong girl or because I didn't see what I had to do to become the right boy, and because those stupid misunderstandings led to me getting my feelings hurt.

There is one exception, though. Her name was Sarah.

Sarah was an Older Woman; she was two grades ahead of me and three years older than me, and even I, the master of self-delusion, couldn't make myself believe I had a chance with her. There are events less common in the universe than a sixteen-year-old girl dating a thirteen-year-old boy—for example, meteor-based mass extinctions—but not too many.

Sarah was a tenth grader who came over to our middle school to be in a play when I was in the eighth grade. Every boy in the cast immediately began orbiting her; she was pretty and vivacious and had boobs and a great smile and would talk to us. For reasons that are still not clear to me, Sarah took a special liking to me. I suspect it's this—some people do theater as teens because it's fun, and some people do it because they have some sort of psychological need to pretend they are someone else. I was definitely in the latter category, and since she continued to be in every play throughout high school (and later transformed from preppy sophomore to patchouli-smelling, black-garment-wearing, Sisters of Mercy–listening semi-goth senior), I assumed Sarah was, too.

Even still, though, the extent to which she not only put up with me but actually liked me was kind of bizarre. Whenever the cast would circle up, Sarah would intentionally sit next to me, or at least put up with me sitting next to her. Our interactions were often flirtatious, which also baffles me in retrospect. I remember sitting behind and above her on the stage's steps, my knees on either side of her rib cage. She was wearing purple Esprit overalls (those of you who did not live through the 1980s will probably be blissfully ignorant of this garment) and it was quite easy for me to peek down the back when she leaned over. So, being an eighth-grade boy, I of course did. "What's Bloomies?" I asked her. "It's written across your butt." She laughed and thought my perviness was cute rather than deeply creepy.

We developed a brief but relatively intense friendship during the months of rehearsal for the play. She was really the first girl I spent hours talking on the phone with. I don't remember a single thing we ever talked about, but I remember monopolizing the phone and my mom being frankly puzzled as to why I was spending so much time talking to this older girl. (That is how she phrased it, though if I were her, I really would have been more puzzled as to why this older girl was spending so much time talking to me. In fact, I'm still kind of puzzled by this.)

This was significant enough, but we also ended up going out a few times—she picked me up at eleven-thirty on a couple of Saturday nights to go downtown for the midnight showing of *The Rocky Horror Picture Show* with her and a bunch of friends. I was a kid whose concept of Saturday night entertainment had, up until this point, consisted of the *The Love Boat/Fantasy Island* double feature on ABC, and suddenly I was thirteen in a car full of sixteen-year-old girls. (Kudos to my mom for saying yes to this! The mists of time have swallowed the memory of how exactly I sold this, but it must have been one hell of a sales job.)

The first time we went to this movie, I sat in the front seat of Sarah's Volkswagen Scirocco (sigh, she drove a sexy car!) while three girls were forced to cram in the back. One of them tried to throw a cigarette out the window, and it landed on my thigh. Sarah yelled at her for me. Another of the girls worried aloud about how she had to get home and clean up beer bottles before her parents returned from their trip the next day. It is safe to say this is the coolest I have ever felt in my entire life.

At the time, people who had never seen the movie were referred to by its cultists as "virgins"—so there were numerous jokes about Sarah taking my virginity on that first night. Certainly these inspired numerous acts of self-love on my part, but they never led me to the delusion that I was in danger of losing my actual virginity, especially to Sarah. This was emphasized in our second trip to the movies, when Sarah got in a fender bender in the Scirocco, and the creepy forty-five-year-old in the other car asked her out in front of me. In my mind, this showed two things: First, Sarah was pretty much an adult, while I was a mere child. Second, this fact was clear to everyone, since it had obviously never occurred to the guy that I was anything but a little brother.

Sarah was, at the time, listening nonstop to the B-52's and Adam and the Ants, and I bought a cassette of the first B-52's album in large part because I worshipped Sarah and she worshipped the B-52's. I liked the simplicity of the music, the wacky sense of humor, and the fact that the music just enraged most of my eighth-grade classmates, most of whom were, as I had been pre-Sarah, still divided into opposing camps of Beatles and Led Zeppelin fans. Everybody met in the middle for The Who, but still it was 1982, and we were all obsessed with bands who, if they still existed at all, had put out their best work when we were all still in diapers. I wish that I saw that my friends were still stuck in the seventies art-rock sensibility and didn't understand the genius of simple pop, but I actually enjoyed the fact that they mocked the music Sarah had introduced me to, because I felt like I got to suffer for love.

I have no doubt that if Sarah had been obsessed with, say, Black Sabbath, I might have gone in a quite different musical direction, but she single-handedly dragged me out of classic rock hell and into new wave, which quickly led to punk. After buying the B-52's cassette just like Sarah's, I went out and bought the Ramones' *End of the Century,* at least partly in hopes of impressing her with my ability to dig weird music that was less than five years old.

Sarah was not especially impressed with the Ramones, but I was. This was the most important musical relationship of my life. The Ramones provided the sound track for my adolescence and remain the one band I love unconditionally. God only knows what band might have filled that void if my desire to impress Sarah hadn't led me to the Ramones. Let's just say it was the 1980s, and the possibilities for horrible musical errors were nearly endless.

I no longer remember how this relationship ended. I know only that, unlike most of my other crushes, there was no terrible, awkward defining moment where I decided to lay my feelings on the line and got them stomped on. It just sort of faded away. I suspect it was just that she was in the tenth grade and I was in the eighth grade, and once we no longer had the play in common, we had less and less in common until it was just kind of weird for her to return my phone calls. (As I said, I don't remember clearly, but I know myself well enough to know there's no way it was me who stopped returning calls from the beautiful older girl.)

The following year, I entered high school, where Sarah was now a junior, and again, sort of uncharacteristically, I made no awkward effort to rekindle our rather strange relationship. This is in part because my relationship with Sarah was so incongruous in my adolescent experience that, unable to make sense of it, my mind just kind of locked it away. I didn't think of it often, and it didn't leave me with any increased confidence about my ability to talk to and spend time with girls. The fact that a really attractive girl had seen fit to hang out with me alone late at night, even in a mascot capacity, did not help see me through the later feelings of heartbreak and despair when I felt sure no girl would ever like me and I would die alone and, more horrifying, a virgin.

Now, though, I can appreciate what I got out of this relationship. There was the music, but more importantly, the lesson I absorbed subconsciously, which was that music geekery was more socially acceptable to most girls than comic book and *Dungeons and Dragons* geekery. (So, in the years following, I could lead with the music geekery and wait till they were hooked to reveal the other kinds.)

My relationship with Sarah was by no means one of the great loves of my life. The emotions didn't run very deep, and whatever there was between us ran its course and then ended. We never fought or disappointed each other, and in the end, neither of us got hurt. So, yeah, it wasn't a real relationship, but that means it was something no real relationship can ever be: perfect.

# Adam

## Amy Greene

I was fifteen the first time I saw Adam. He was driving across the high school parking lot in a black Mustang convertible with a white ragtop. I had never seen anyone in a convertible before. Most of the people I knew drove pickup trucks. I lived on a back road surrounded by pastures with the mountains a chain of ridged humps in the distance. I grew up on a farm passed down through generations of our family, in a frame house my grandfather built. I went to a rural elementary school with kids whose parents were farmers or factory workers like mine. But high school was a jarring change for me. Each morning I was bused to the crowded brick school building in town, where my classmates didn't wear hand-me-downs or shoes caked with field mud. Right away, I felt the difference between myself and them. I learned to be ashamed of what I didn't have and the rusted-out cars my parents drove, bought only to get from one place to another. Maybe that's why Adam's convertible stirred something in me. It seemed impractical, made for joyriding. When the girl sitting across from me in world geography class confessed to having a crush on Adam, I said, "You can have him and I'll take his car."

Then one day he stood up in the auditorium after a school play and turned around to smile at someone else. I was struck by the handsomeness of his face. It was a secret, fleeting moment that I forgot about until later. But he meant something different to me after that. Even at a glance, I could tell there was something special about him. I took note of his passage in the halls without making an effort to talk to him. At the time, I always walked with my head down and my shoulders bowed, uncomfortable in my own skin. I didn't realize how much alike Adam and I were. He was creative, an artist who liked to draw and read and write. I think about us being in the same building without knowing it, both of us miserable. If we'd found each other sooner, maybe we could have been happier. Maybe we wouldn't look back on high school and hate it so much.

We became acquainted when he dated my best friend for a while. One day after they broke up, he offered to take me home from school. I said no, as much as I had come to like him. I was ashamed of our small, weathered house, how far out of town it was and how old the falling-down barn in the back field was and the slow cows grazing behind barbwire. But he was persistent, and when I finally gave in, we talked so much on the way that I barely noticed I was riding in his convertible. I forgot to be ashamed of where I lived. I learned that I had been right about him. He was different, like me. We talked about things I hadn't been able to with anyone else my age, the stories we were dreaming up and the books we liked and what we thought about the world outside of the mountains.

After that first ride we went everywhere together. We took walks down dirt roads and railroad tracks and into the woods behind my house, sharing things with each other that no one else understood. We rode with the top down into the hills, between fields and over creek water, the wind sweet with honeysuckle. His black Mustang with a white ragtop became part of our relationship, a catalyst for the real love that was growing between us.

Then one night the engine blew up while we were on the way for ice cream. Smoke poured from under the hood in dark billows. I was afraid we would be stranded on the side of the road, but somehow we made it back to his house. We were able to laugh about the situation, as sad as it was to see the Mustang parked in the high grass of the lot next door. Adam borrowed an Escort with a bad muffler to make the long drive from town to my house. After that, I listened for him with one ear through my open window and it was hard getting used to the sound of a strange car. But the important thing was him getting to me.

For a long time Adam's Mustang sat in the weedy lot with the ragtop mildewing and the rain getting in. He worked at a fast-food restaurant, frying fish, but what he made wasn't enough to have the engine overhauled. When I graduated high school, I took half the money I was given to fix the car and the other half to buy a wedding dress. By then we knew we were getting married, even though I was eighteen and he was twenty. Nothing could have changed our minds. We loved each other too much.

On our wedding day cans rattled behind us as we pulled away from the little white church in the valley where we got married, less than a mile from the house I grew up in. We headed for the mountains, and when Adam stopped to pump gas, the bigness of what we had done swelled up in me. I had married my first love.

We had the same last name. He would be my only love now. Adam took me home from our weekend honeymoon in the Smokies to the tiny garage apartment we had rented. When he went off to work, I opened the window and listened for the sound of the Mustang bringing him back to me.

Before I even got the hang of being a wife, I found out that I was going to be a mother. We looked at the Mustang, ours now, and knew that we couldn't keep a car made for joyriding. Adam put an ad in the newspaper and a teenage girl called about buying it. She wanted it to be her first car. I liked the idea of her having it but her father wouldn't buy it for her. I wonder where it is now, if it even runs anymore. I can't much picture it running without us. We have been married for almost sixteen years and have driven many vehicles with no sentimental value. Their only purpose is to get us from one place or another. But it was never about the car, anyway. It has always been about Adam and me.

Getting married young wasn't the easiest road we could have taken. But all that we've learned has been worth any of the challenges we faced. Maybe the most important lesson for me was that it's okay to be proud of who I am and where I come from. Adam showed me that. Since the afternoon he drove me home from school, we've taught each other a lot. We've grown up and found ourselves together. I love the person Adam has become as much as the boy he was when we first met. We have a busy life now as writers and parents, but we still make time for long rides in the country with the windows down, between fields and over creek water. Now that we have two kids in the back, the honeysuckle only smells sweeter on the wind.

# My Romantic Past (or, What I Heard on My Relationship): A Mix Tape

## Emily Franklin

*Songs are never quite the answer/Just a soundtrack to a life...*
—Badly Drawn Boy

Maybe it's the early eighties and I'm dancing with Brad only because my mother made him ask me. He's my brother's best-looking friend who will later defy everyone's vision for his life as a cardiologist by becoming a ski bum in Boulder or Denver, some rocky place I won't visit. The song is "Hot Child in the City" and we're at my brother's bar mitzvah and for two minutes and thirty-three seconds, I have a boyfriend. More importantly, and longer lasting, is the jukebox entry for this song. Doesn't matter who sings it, really, because what the song is now—for me—is that hot afternoon in late spring with my new flats scuffing the makeshift stage and hand-me-down skirt flowing as Brad gyrates and rolls his eyes at his friends.

The point: each relationship (and the definition of this word is open to debate) can be distilled into one song. Not the song you necessarily want it to be, but the one that reverberates in your heart when you think back to the first time you laughed hard enough together that you thought, *This is what I want to do all the time,* or when you pressed your bodies together, or how you found yourself broken up with right before your brother's wedding and his best man/friend said, "Yeah, I thought you guys would get married, too." But I'm getting ahead of myself.

This is one of those annoying mixes that feels too personal, like you're missing the hidden message in each song. Except that everyone has a mix like this (and if you don't now, you will) even if the playlist differs, even if your list wouldn't be caught dead hanging with my Smiths and Stevie Wonder, wouldn't dance with my Tears for Fears or look twice at my Steely Dan or recognize my Voice of the Beehive as a band rather than an improbable statistical phrase. Playlists and CDs erase one wonderful aspect that the cassette tape had: side A and side B. Used to be, you could have a built-in before and after, a marker of time or issues, of boys to men or pre- to postcollege. But we don't have that anymore. So here is A and B...and everything in between.

**"Everybody Wants to Rule the World"—Tears for Fears.**
Jaret. Jared? Jarrett. We get together because, and this is reason enough when you are thirteen, we are romantic leads in the camp play. Don't remember the title, something about a superhero. Jared is not from Krypton; he is from New Jersey. After we kiss for the first and only time, he leaves behind a letter he's writing to his folks back in the Garden State that says, in part, "And she's not bad looking, either!"

**"Sledgehammer"—Peter Gabriel.** It's fall of freshman year of high school and I'm lured to the art room by a boy with prep school hair and a wicked grin who will later go on to shave his head for the military but who right now, with Peter Gabriel blasting through the open windows, delivers a stunning few kisses before returning me to my chattering friends. I had noticed Sam before the art room, of course, but hadn't thought he'd seen me, what with his cooler, older friends who used words like *abecedarian* and *dehisce* in their everyday speech. The art room kiss breaks the spell of my crush on Sam, but my crush on the words lingers.

**"Only a Dream in Rio"—James Taylor.** Part of me believes siblings exist partially to provide a dating pool. Or pond. Summer again and older brother's BFF makes a tape with too much 1970s guitar and not enough lyrics for me to overinterpret. Despite this, we wind up making out at the James Taylor concert outside. He has a crush on me, he says, but one that can't lead to anything, because he's older and, besides, the concert is almost over. I'm left sure that friendship is a key component of my ideal, but where to fit that into a crush or romance.

**"Sheila Take a Bow"—The Smiths.** Maybe I don't need any coffee this morning. Maybe I've already had it but maybe I want to see if you're working at the coffee place today, and since you are, I can't just go in and stare at you and leave, so I have to use my last two dollars to buy coffee I don't really want to see if you have eyeliner on with your black T-shirt or if you're just spiking your hair and mouthing the words to this song. Do you even know I'm here? Yes, when I spill my coffee and wipe out trying to clean it up.

**"I Say Nothing"—Voice of the Beehive.** If there's one person not to have a crush on, it's your best friend's new guy friend, which is too bad because at the aquarium he makes me laugh so hard apple juice comes out my nose, which only solidifies the attraction for both of us. If I'd known then that you had an identical twin, maybe the problem could have been solved by simple math, but instead, we plunge into secrecy, into holding hands in the dark where she can't see, into phone calls and stolen kisses and so much guilt that we tell her and it's worse than if we'd just kept it to ourselves and said nothing. Still, the song is upbeat despite the cloaked issues, and the bounce lasts when the tape ends.

**"Sign Your Name"—Terence Trent D'Arby.** Where are you now, David #1? Looking back, you could have been a real love of mine had I not let myself get distracted by studying abroad. And by studying abroad I mean writing some terrible poems and one good essay about art and having some guy named Neil declare his love for me by puking the contents of his six-foot-five-inch frame out in my tiny Oxford room. Whenever this song starts up, the notes carry with it missed opportunity. You were funny, smart and looked adorable in your plaid boxers and collegiate T-shirt worn so thin it was butter soft when we said goodbye.

**"Gimme Some Lovin'"—Spencer Davis Group.** Dancing school hell is lessened only by the fact that my mother lets me borrow her drop-waist black dress and by Steven Y., who for some reason dances only with me. Too bad he's from a different high school, because he knows all the words to this. To be honest, this song is cross-referenced with a non-romantic part of my life. When I gave birth to my first child, I took an infant CPR class. All the new parents sat on the floor with their dummy children while the real ones napped or cried in their car seats and the young instructor tried to teach the timing of CPR—when to blow into the mouth, when to do chest compressions. "I can't get the hang of this," my friend Heather said, blushing as her fake baby failed to breathe. "Hey," I whispered to her, "just think of 'Gimme Some Lovin'…opening line…bum-bum-bum-bum-bum-*press!*" Our dummy babies got in the groove. Steve Y. moved back to Bermuda and I never wrote him back.

**"Skateaway"—Dire Straits.** First love comes out of nowhere. One minute I'm a high school junior and the next I'm like the girl in the song, with wheels on my feet, skating alongside Dave. Not literally. He would no sooner roller-skate than he would express himself in public. My days are spent mooning through math class, chucking quarters into the pay phone—the jangle of change is its own romantic music, dwindling as the months go by. There are tapes sent and parents met and love pledged and sushi eaten, and a crushed heart (mine) and a song that will never be the same no matter how many years or decades have rushed by. The misty edges of crushdom expand into solid form, and it's impossible not to be changed.

**"This Must Be the Place"—Talking Heads.** What is it with me and the Canadians? While learning French, Ron the Gardener (long hair, irreverent humor, infinite U2 knowledge) makes me a mix, and even now, when I'm shuttling four children around in my minivan, I am transported back to that rose-filled garden, those nights that exist only when you're seventeen and stretch into the next morning.

**"Enjoy the Silence"—Depeche Mode.** When I tell my mom about my crush on the waiter, she asks why I must find love only in the service professions—gardeners, cooks, no janitors yet. When will I find someone from whom I can learn and not only teach? Ian and I spend the summer lusting after each other as my crush blossoms into whatever comes between crush and love. Like, I suppose. We like each other a lot. He resembles no one so much as an older Peter Pan (minus the tights). He teaches me to roll my own cigarettes (see, Mom, they *can* teach me stuff), and when we find each other on Facebook so many years later, he looks exactly the same and the song plays in an endless loop, somehow erasing the negative parts of the relationship—the pregnancy scare, the falling out of touch, and the time he biked all the way to London and came to my first big party even though he knew no one and I virtually ignored him the way quiet seeps into people when they have nothing left to offer.

**"Sensitive Artist"—King Missile.** Dear Bad College Poet in the Dorm Next Door, I saw you again today from my second-floor room, you in bare feet on the road, looking at a bird or a telephone wire or perhaps nothing but wanting to appear focused on something far away. And then you saw me and I ducked. Yes, self-esteem is a good thing, but in moderation. Your sonnets are grating but your hair is pretty and long as in the fashion of the nineties. Your demeanor is crafted so as to appear timeless. Also, you wear vests a lot and eat Pop-Tarts as an ironic gesture. You loathe me because you are competitive and because I commented on how you've worn the same wool sweater for five weeks straight. But I meant it in a good way, like your art elevates your needs above material desires. But you think too much of yourself to allow my humor to penetrate your poetic exterior. Butterflies nest in your hair, angels in your pockets, you of the gliding walk and vampire white smile. Just so you know, I have a crush on you even though I also kind of hate you or at least hate myself for crushing.

**"Last Train Home"—Pat Metheny.** You think the crushes you get as a teenager will amount to simple memories. But for me, like this song, with its chugging jazz and twanging guitar, a few circled back around. The holiday romance that no one thought would last away from that Greek island resulted in letters and visits and phone calls in Italian when I learned to speak it. And isn't that what the songs are, and what love is, learning fluency in another person's language? Years would go by and the song would disappear from my radar and then show up out of nowhere in some boutique or on the college radio station. It haunted me off and on, right up until the proposal, at which point it became clear that the future I flirted with—me as the American writer in Italy, you as the surgeon in Milan—was for me only a flirtation.

**"Wicked Game"—Chris Isaak.** You want this to be our song, so it is. Never really liked it all that much, but I loved you pretty much from the New Year's Eve party when we met and you told me I looked like one of the Three Musketeers in my leggings and boots. Three years, miles of flights and that drive across country when I wanted to sing terrible hits from the 1970s but you wanted Genesis and Aja, so we compromised and listened to nothing as America streamed by the windows.

**"Two Tickets to Paradise"—Eddie Money.** In which we meet at the very end of college and embark on what should be a great summer fling but which turns into the relationship that defines my early twenties. To be continued....

**"Walking on Broken Glass"—Annie Lennox.** No one ever told me that love should be easy. And the way you hold yourself and your heart back from me makes me chase it down. I didn't realize it at the time, but having a crush on you back in college—a mutual crush—was gentle. Lovely, even. But in the expanse of the adult world shone our rough spots. You teach me to need you, which I will have to unlearn later, but also provide me with other skills. I learn how to make bread from scratch, how to cook for forty at a time without so much as flinching, how if you hurt yourself (with a hot pan or a dropped wooden log on your toe, say) the best thing to do is to shoulder through it.

**"Signed, Sealed, Delivered I'm Yours"—Stevie Wonder.** After the big grown-up relationship ends, I meet you. I have a crush on you before I even meet you, having been filled in by my friend who is your apartment mate in London. "He is perfect for what you need right now" which meant he was gorgeous and funny and took my mind off my previous relationships. We are the casual crush incarnate—fun dinners, romantic strolls in old English gardens, and no painful goodbyes, just fading out when it's time to leave.

**"Kiss of Life"—Sade.** Thanks again, older brother, for giving me a prince. Okay, fine, he's a count. But still. Everyone should have one really fun date with royalty in which your date brings you a rose, takes you to dinner, and then you tromp through London to an impossibly posh party with champagne flutes and well-heeled elite, only to find that you've stumbled into the wrong party.

Everyone, though, is so charming that we stay for one more round before dancing without music in the moonlight and greeting the morning together. The prince/count/viscount/earl/lord calls work to feign sickness so the date can continue over breakfast.

**"I'll Know"—from the *Guys and Dolls* sound track.** Four hours into our meeting and your friends ask if we're going to get married. The answer is yes but we don't believe it yet because we're just playing Ping-Pong and singing songs from musicals and sharing our life histories and cracking up because I don't like keeping score and you're obsessed with it. My crush develops as the ball pings and pongs from one side of the green table to the other, but when you ask me out, I have to decline. I say I'm leaving to hike in India and Nepal. Even though this is true, it sounds like an elaborate excuse. You say you're going to Ecuador to practice rural medicine and this sounds like the match point. Really, though, I am scared by my crush—do you feel the same way? Across the table at dinner, I wonder if years from now, when I look back on the inevitable sound track of my romantic life, if yours will be the song I regret most. The crush that I pocket like a lucky penny, like a wish. But you, true to your spirit and to the song that insists you'll know when your love comes along, you ask again in a letter and this time I don't let it go. I jump on a plane and three months after we meet, eighty-five thousand miles of travel later, we are married. And the song was right.

So concludes the sound track. I know more things now; *dehisce* means to burst open, like a milkweed pod when it's ripe, and an *abecedarian* is one who is learning the alphabet. My last crush was my biggest, my most important, and every day now, with my late thirties adult life in full swing with four young children and a career and house, I still have a crush. When my children ask about love, about long-term partnership, I will tell them this: You have to have a crush on your spouse. You must feel as though you can't believe your luck that this person, your ultimate crush, feels exactly the same way.

# The Subtle Art
# of Crush-Suffocating

## Joshua Mohr

"How's your stalker?" says a buddy of mine, Michael. I'm not changing his name, because he's sort of an asshole.

"She's not a stalker. It's just a crush."

"She's a stalker."

"She likes my writing."

"Your writing? That's the stupidest thing I've ever heard," he says.

This woman—let's call her Carrie—often lingered after the writing workshop I led to ask questions. But this particular time she had some presents, beautifully gift-wrapped. Keep in mind that it was nowhere near my birthday or Christmas or Kwanzaa or a rogue bar mitzvah.

She smiled, handed them to me. "These aren't exactly for you."

"No?"

"They're for Rhonda."

Carrie was being cute. Rhonda is the male narrator from my first novel, *Some Things That Meant the World to Me*.

We were alone at this point, the other students long gone.

"Rhonda?" I said, playing along like an imbecile.

"Open them up, silly," she said.

But if we back up a bit, there's more to this. There's everything I've ignored. The warning signs that a teacher with more experience than me would have handled gracefully. So smooth and discreet, with such aplomb, these veteran instructors would have realigned the relationship into something more suitable without Carrie even noticing.

But I've been teaching for only three years. I am thirty-four years old. I haven't yet honed these chops at the subtle art of crush-suffocating. I am the sort of person that sees the path of least resistance (in this case pretending that there is no real crush at all). I see this path and think to myself, *Well now, obviously, it would be best for everyone if I just pretend like nothing's going on....*

Yeah, I'm that dumb.

This fact was not lost on my girlfriend, Fiona.

"You have to say something to her," she said, unimpressed with my let-sleeping-dogs-lie attitude.

"It will pass."

"Will it?"

"Of course. Probably. I'm dealing with it."

"How exactly are you dealing with it?" she asked. Let me emphasize her *unimpressedness*.

♥♥♥

The first assignment Carrie ever turned in to me, the first red flag—it was a short story in which I was a main character, starring opposite…wait for it…wait…starring opposite Carrie! It was a sci-fi love story set somewhere in the future.

I give written feedback on all student submissions. I can't tell you exactly what I said to her—some crap about it being an interesting fictionalization of real life and other shoddy teacher double-speak.

But I can tell you what I didn't write. There was no mention of me being creeped out. Or the fact that I didn't feel it was appropriate. Or for the first time, I felt uncomfortable around a student. I didn't say any of a hundred things that would have accurately conveyed my feelings to her, or given Carrie the opportunity to hear an articulation of my unease.

Instead, in perfect coward form, I probably handed it back to her and said something asinine like, "Good job."

I don't think I'm terrified of confrontation (unless that in and of itself represents a sort of conflict I thrive in evading). I've had plenty of uncomfortable conversations over the years. So what about Carrie? Why couldn't I talk to her about how she was making me feel?

Kicking it over now, I think it has something to do with the possibility that I worried I might have been wrong. What if Carrie's behavior, while a bit presumptuous, didn't have anything to do with a crush? What if I was making a mountain out of a molehill? How embarrassing, I rationalized, to broach this topic, only to find out that it was all arrogant extrapolation on my part.

I ran this theory of self-conspiracy by Fiona.

"Please, for my own peace of mind," she said, "tell me you aren't this dense."

"Of course not."

In retrospect, I should've asked her to clarify.

Oh, wait, I never told you the gifts that Carrie gave to me for Rhonda. They were all framed from items featured in the novel: a food Rhonda enjoyed eating, the root ingredients for a Bloody Maria, miscellaneous stickers depicting background details from the book's settings.

"Thanks so much," I said to her, grinning with a cluster of apprehension and hubris and greed. "This is really great."

This is really great? What the hell was I talking about?

The point of this isn't to make fun of Carrie, to demean or target her feelings. Far from it. The point is to examine my part in this crush, if that's even what it was.

By not establishing a sturdy boundary, was I participating, was I encouraging her? Did I like the attention?

In the midst of my monogamy, was I getting a vicarious orgasm from all this?

These are gross questions. Ones that stink of the sort of self-awareness that I don't possess. I chose the path of least resistance with Carrie, the easy way out. I chose to play ridiculously dumb to her body language, the presents, her story where we shared the stage. My "logic" was basic: our class would end. That would be that. Problem solved. Our worlds would separate.

Until she enrolled in my class the following session.

♥♥♥

They say those in glass houses can't cast stones, so it's only fair for me to mention the time I "stalked" Denis Johnson. He's one of my favorite writers, and a buddy of mine was hosting two days of Denis's readings and lectures down at San José State.*

Anyway, Fiona and I drove down from San Francisco for Denis's evening reading. Then we crashed a party where I cornered my ol' buddy Denis and forced him to answer my self-enterprising questions. Then Fiona and I got a motel room and were back at San José State bright and early for a noontime Q & A. Then—and here's where things get a bit "weird"—we followed my chum Denis into a graduate seminar where he talked fiction with ten people (twelve, if you count F. and me). Despite our unofficial presence, I asked even more self-enterprising questions.

Afterward, we drove home, ecstatic, not feeling the least bit creepy.

It's not until we share our Denis-centric itinerary with friends that we understand our borderline stalker status.

"What's the big deal?" we said.

"The big deal is following a stranger around for two days," they said.

"It was nothing. He wasn't bothered by it."

"How do you know?"

We didn't know, of course. I won't speak for Fiona here, but I will say this: I was basing my feelings that Denis wasn't bothered on his sweeping ambivalence to our presence. We were specks of

---

* *I'm going to call him Denis even though I don't know him. Isn't that Stalker 101, establishing inappropriate intimacy with your mark?*

dust. Barely there. In all likelihood, he never knew we were the only people attending all his events, invited or not.

And if he was bothered, the path of least resistance worked. He ignored us, treated us like any other sycophants. The day ended. He went back to his life and we went back to ours.

So certainly the same thing would happen to Carrie, right? She couldn't take my classes forever (could she?). Life would go on and we'd be in our own sovereign status quos.

I was nervous before the first class began. Uneasy. But still there was no plan anywhere.

I couldn't stomach saying something like, "Carrie, your behavior isn't being respectful of our predisposed power dynamic."

Or: "Carrie, I think you're a special girl, but please, we need to maintain a professional boundary."

Blah...

No way.

Too scary to be that adult.

And then the moment of truth...or the moment of cowardice... or the moment of something...

Carrie came in. She sat down. We chatted briefly about what she'd been writing and the class began. There was no weirdness whatsoever.

Wait.

That's not right. That's not true.

There was weirdness. Of course, there was weirdness.

The thing was, though, it didn't exist between Carrie and me. It was all happening in my skull. I was the weirdness. I didn't know what to do and I didn't know what to say. These rollicking questions staggered through me like drunkards and I was tripping over my words. Carrie was perfectly calm, which made me stammer even more, and I was sweating and she wasn't sweating. She was all smiles and calmness. "Are you okay?" she asked and I said, "I need some coffee," and she said, "You and your coffee." She was normal and I was a cluster of weirdness but then someone else asked me something and I got busy talking to him and more people came in and soon our class started and then our class ended and she was the first to leave.

"I think I made the whole thing up," I said to Fiona later.
"No, you didn't."
"It seems over."
"Does it?"
"I think. Yeah. She was totally normal. Like any other student. It was weird."
"What was weird?"
"I don't know yet," I said. "But it felt weird."
"We'll see if the dam holds," she said.

And that's basically it. The dam—as Fiona put it—was constructed solidly. It held the whole time. No weird gifts or stories where I populated the page. The crush was over or dormant or she'd realized that I had seen a glimpse of it and hadn't been interested. Or she realized that *she* wasn't interested the more she got to know me as more than just a classroom persona. Or some other possibility I'm too oblivious to ponder.

I, at the very least, expected some hyperbolic goodbye between us as the last class ended. But nothing. A hug. That was all.

A hug and she walked out and I was left with a feeling of tangled relief. A lonely feeling of emotional masturbation.

♥♥♥

I read in Berkeley recently and saw Carrie there for the first time in months. I kissed her cheek. We exchanged stock pleasantries. It was a benign moment, a nice moment actually.

Either the crush had been a figment of my narcissism or her affections had now moved on to someone else. Or these things have a natural course to run, and once through the maze, the impossibility of their reality becomes too much to ignore. There probably isn't one clean, tidy answer. Jesus, wouldn't our lives be easier with clean, tidy answers?

Sometimes, we intrude into each other's worlds. Sometimes we follow Denis Johnson around and pelt him with questions. Or we give presents to people that they don't receive as innocuous affections, but gift-wrapped ulterior motives. Why do we do these things? Where does that gaudy drive come from?

As for Carrie and me (and probably you, too, if you're willing to be honest about it), it's hard to respect other people's boundaries because they're different for all of us. At our best moments, we try and honor vague ideas of what may infringe into another person's safety zone. At our most selfish, we shove our own aspirations into the foreground. What makes it all so tricky is that there are no fixed delineations. Nothing we can view as a map or rule book. No way to eavesdrop into the hearts and minds of strangers to glean their comfort levels.

So we do the best we can: We make the rules up as we go along. We hopefully try to live lives that don't bother others. And if we do breach this indefinable division, we catch our straying sooner rather than later. It's better to realize this on our own before Denis Johnson grabs us by the collar and yells in our face, "Why won't you mind your own business? Who do you think you are? Just what gives you the right to bully into my life like this?"

Because those savage questions leave us no choice but to contemplate how our harmless itinerary led us into volatile territory. And we stand there wondering when our delusions got so splendid and conniving and ornate.

# Olfactory

## Catherine Newman

If I could tell this story to you as a scratch-and-sniff book, then you might really get it. And it would start with Macy's Herald Square in the spring of 1985. There would be an illustration of my mom and me on the escalator, and you would scratch and sniff the perfume counters: Giorgio, Anaïs Anaïs, Lauren—the smell of the rich girls at my high school, of my teenagerhood, of that very store where my dad worked, where we're on our way up to the juniors department to buy me a swimsuit. The perfume is like a fog: it's in our hair, saturating our clothes, and filling our nostrils. But also I'm holding my fingers up to my face, clenching and unclenching them to smell my own born-again hands. I am burning, burning, burning and my heart is going to explode and what I have is a secret and what I am is in love.

Actually, it wouldn't start there. Maybe it would start with the drummers: Chris Partridge (sigh) and, later, Larry Mullen, Jr. from

U2 (sigh), only there wouldn't be any scratching or sniffing here, because they were on TV. You could ogle their faces and biceps, and you could *imagine* what they smelled like (Johnson's baby shampoo or hairy Irish tank-top armpits)—but, sadly, you couldn't actually smell them. I was like our cat: when we try to interest him in photographs of other cats—without the aromatic provocation of fur, paws, a butt to sniff—he looks for a while and then he yawns and looks away.

But turn past that page of drummers, and now it's 1981. Can you see me in my lace-and-ribbon Gunne Sax blouse, my fine-wale khaki corduroy knickers and Kork-Ease sandals (with socks)? There, at a bar mitzvah dance party, swaying under the disco ball with Cute Boy? Scratch and sniff his silky hair. That's Prell.

Now comes an entire chapter—the years 1982–1984—of high school X-Country Boy, and every page smells the same. X-Country Boy! It was the era of unrequitedness, my diary like a navigational logbook of the boy's every movement, his every set of schoolhouse coordinates: lockers, American history, cafeteria, track. Did he notice me or not notice me? Talk to me or not talk to me? All of this was noted diligently, daily. His apartment building was two blocks from mine, and I knew the yellow-lit square of his bedroom window. I knew his clean T-shirts and smooth face, his pink cheeks and the blond hair falling over his eyes. I knew his downy forearms better than I knew my own. But mostly what I knew was his laundry-detergent smell. I know it still: I catch that powdery exhalation from a basement vent or a friend's embrace, and I am flooded by the tsunami of nostalgia, sucked in by an undertow of longing. Is that why they call it *Tide?*

Childhood had been the smell of hamsters and our dad's True cigarettes, vanilla and baby powder and cherry Sucrets.

College would be the smell of dirty sheets, morning breath and black coffee. But teenaged lust was the smell of laundry: all, Cheer, Fab. We were half-formed: so grown that we might grind together the damp crotches of our clean Levi's; so young that those jeans were laundered still by our moms, folded in warm piles at the foot of our beds when we got home from school. My spin-cycle crushes were worse than ring around the collar: the more you scrubbed them, the more indelible they became.

Oh, crushes. *Crush* is a funny word. It sounds so innocent: bubbly orange soda, or maybe a barrel of Chianti grapes mashed comically underfoot. But then suddenly it's so heavy: you're Wile E. Coyote in a Road Runner cartoon, and there's an anvil falling on your head; you're walking below the window that a piano is tumbling out of; you're smashed flat by pheromones; you're a teenaged girl with a boy on top of you, pressing from your very cells the juice of yearning. The smell of it.

Ah, look! Here's the Macy's page—but we're going to skip past it for right now. We're going to read ahead into the future: sweet-tart memories all cataloged by odor. Scratch and sniff that next picture: the girl, sitting naked on a kitchen stool and shoveling into her ravenous person the spaghetti *aglio e olio* that her teen-aged lover has prepared for her. It's 1986. Can you smell the garlic? Can you smell the sex? I could. "We could die happy," we said, and meant it. We were like Romeo and Juliet, star-crossed by the fact that our parents were, tragically, often at home.

1987. College. Vain Boy told me that I smelled like juice oranges, which was sexy, and Bazooka bubble gum, which we chewed a lot of together. He himself smelled of Noxzema, the assiduous use of which prevented me from ever once falling asleep in his arms: he leapt nightly from loving to scrub his pretty face. "I can't skip a night," he explained, "or I'll break out." Mentholated clove is still, for me, the smell of waiting. Of being left.

Buddha Boy smelled like nag champa and Right Guard stick deodorant and grubby Ultimate Frisbee bandanas. Fiction Girl smelled—surprise!—like a girl. Lacan Boy smelled like Marlboros and Redhook Ale, man sweat and the shag carpet of his beachside motel apartment. We inhaled the Pacific fog that blew into his windows all night alongside the achy barking of the seal lions. They wanted, wanted, wanted something—that's what it sounded like. To me, at least.

We're going to get back to Macy's, we are. Because the rest? It's a different story entirely. I will meet the love of my life, whose face will smell like Old Spice, like my dad's. We will wander into town to buy and eat discounted Easter chocolates: "Oh, was it Easter?" we will say languidly to each other, disoriented by the blurring of day and night, passionately wasted. I will put my nose to his worn jean jacket, to his Bart Simpson T-shirt, to his dark hair and the warm skin of his neck, and I will know that I am home.

But that's years away. Now I am just a girl still—a daughter out shopping with her mom. Only I'm something else, too. Because just yesterday I was sharing a package of Twinkies with my beautiful boyfriend on the subway after a track meet, both of us high off of running and Yoo-hoo and the knowledge that we were going home to an empty apartment. The IRT juddered and steamed around us in the spring twilight while we held hands and barely spoke. I was wearing my lucky fake pearls, and later that night I wore only those pearls, and I was lucky, lucky, lucky. We were in our underwear in my parents' bed with the television on, and Madonna was singing "Crazy for You" on MTV, which we heard but didn't see because we were blub-blubbing down in the deep, looking and looking into each other's brown eyes, our own green eyes, we didn't even know. And then there was no more laundry smell. There was only the briny-sweet smell of his brown skin, and I was blacking out with desire so new I didn't even recognize it. "I think I'm sick," I said, shivering underneath him, and he pushed the hair out of my face and kissed me. "I think you're crushing me," I said. I hadn't known it would be so muscular. So hard. We were slick with sweat and with something else, maybe, that smelled like the ocean that was roaring in my ears. "I've never felt like this before," I said—or someone sang it from the TV—and he said, "Me, either."

Now I'm standing in a navy blue Speedo in the fitting room, and my mother is smiling at me, and I can't help wondering if she can see it on my skin. If she can smell it. Because I can, only I don't even understand if what's on my hands is him or me. I am new even to myself. Of course, that same smell will blur into other relationships, other romances; it will not be unique to this moment. And far into the future, its brackish primacy will be overtaken by the blood and milk, the sweat and tears of parenthood: we will press our faces to the fragrant scalps of the babies, and our hearts will fly up out of our bodies like unstrung helium balloons. Love will fill us up and spill over and we won't be able to grasp it. We can't grasp it still. But in a department store, even now, that fragrant squall of perfume can flatten me. Tea rose and grapefruit, lily, bergamot and musk. It smells like the start of something: something so microscopically small you can breathe it into your lungs, and so vast that it transforms the world.

# Uncle Greg, a Giant Chicken, and the Murderous Pottery Wheel

## Heather Swain

Uncle Greg was my first crush, of my first semester, of my first year of college. Before you think I'm some inbred hick, let me set the record straight: I might be from a teeny farm town in the middle of Indiana, but Greg was not related to me by blood. Nope. In my mind, he was sent to me by those whimsical gods of love who have nothing better to do than muck with a freshman's head. Now, two decades later, I'm about to track him down again.

I'd first seen him through the large Plexiglas cereal dispensers in the dorm cafeteria. Was it the slight curls of his shaggy brown hair or those piercing eyes or the confident, maybe even cocky, way he loped around with his tray in one hand? Or maybe that he seemed infinitely more interesting than the farm boys I grew up with and I wanted something different than football, cars and beer bongs in my next boyfriend.

Today in the cyberworld, I don't have to inhabit the same physical space as he does to see him again. This time, I turn to the internet. First I Google him, which turns up a professional photo (same eyes, same sort of cocky disposition, still cute) but my search doesn't render an email address, so I do what any twenty-first-century gal would do: I Facebook him.

Where was Facebook when I was in college? It would have been a handy shortcut. Back then dorky girls like me had to do reconnaissance for one another.

Through my friends, I learned that Greg was a journalism major, wrote for the school newspaper and took French. Obviously, we were meant for one another because the point would not be the common ground between us, anyway. It would be all the new things we could bring to one another. If only I could find a way to do more than squeak, "Um, hi," and scurry away like a spastic chipmunk whenever I passed him on the quad.

Today I have the luxury of a keyboard and time delay to craft my message to Greg, but as I get up my gumption to "talk" to him, many of the feelings are the same as when I was eighteen. Am I being weird? Will he think I'm a freak? Will he know who I am? I call my friend Emily and we giggle like tweens while parsing every word of my message, which reminds me of being in middle school and writing notes on lined paper to boys. Which is ridiculous because I'm forty years old, happily married, and have no interest in this person other than to get his side of the story about an ill-fated date in college. And yet, I remain a dorky girl at heart who's afraid I'll embarrass myself (again) after all these years.

In the email, I reintroduce myself and explain that we went to college together. Then I tell him that I'm writing an essay about crushes and he's my subject. Like usual, I go on for too long (in real-time conversation this is known as nervous babbling). I overexplain things, add disclaimers and justifications (and use far too many parentheses) while generally talking myself into circles. Then at the end, I ask him to please contact me. And I wait.

Back in my college dorm, while I was waiting around, trying to figure out a way to approach him, providence struck. The guys in our dorm had a fund-raiser. For what, I have no idea. Homeless puppies? A big fat kegger? Who knew, but that wasn't the point. For a mere five dollars you could buy a bedtime story and two guys would come to your dorm room to tuck you in. My roommate and I quickly ponied up our fiver.

The night of our tucking in rolled around and Jill and I spent as much time primping as we did getting ready for class in the morning. With our hair in appropriately messy ponytails and in our cutest pj's, we were ready for the 9:00 p.m. knock at the door. But nothing could have prepared me for my crush walking into our room.

"Hey there," my crush said, one hand in his faded jeans pocket, the other holding a sheaf of loose-leaf paper. "I'm Uncle Greg and this is Uncle Todd and we're here to tuck you in." Then, they both doubled over in that I-just-smoked-a-giganto-bong kind of laugh where absolutely everything, especially whatever you happen to be doing, is hilarious. Including reading a nonsense story they'd scribbled down while they were toking it up fifteen minutes earlier.

Oh, but it didn't matter! He was there, in my room, and he was delicious. Even cuter close up than I had thought. And what a great laugh he had! Plus, he clearly knew how to have fun. So what if I never did drugs or drank? I could be the designated driver.

A few days later, on the way to the cafeteria, I saw him. The conversation went something like this:

Me (all moony-eyed and swooning while feigning casual self-confidence): "Oh hey, Uncle Greg."

Him (Look of bewilderment as to why I could call him Uncle).

Me (slightly flustered but pushing forward, anyhow): "You, um, read me and my roommate a bedtime story the other night?" My voice crept up and up until it was more like a question.

Him (look of vague recognition): "Oh yeah, right, I was really baked that night."

And then what? All I could do was give him a meek half wave and scurry off once again, as if I had to quickly hide an acorn in some underground burrow. Oh, but it hurt, because to him, coming to my dorm room had been a lark, while to me it had been divine intervention. And since I was painfully shy at the time, I couldn't find a way to talk to him again and so the years passed.

I dated other people, spent my summers working on an island in the Great Lakes, went to London for my junior year, and then returned to my college for my senior year a new person. I had decided in London to no longer be shy. I set a challenge for myself. I would do the things in life that made me afraid, because otherwise I was missing too much fun. (I still live by this rubric, which is why I sent Greg the email.)

Once I was back on campus, I started reading the university newspaper. Every week I found myself interested in what a reporter named Greg had to say. And yes, dear reader, it was the one and only Uncle Greg. Once again those crazy love gods were toying with me, were they not? Only this time the new Heather would not sit back and pine away, letting life pass me by.

I decided that if I couldn't find a way to talk to him, then I would find other means of communication.

Since this was long before email, let alone virtual social networking, I went old school and wrote to him. Being an aspiring fiction writer, I wrote him a short story. It was no ordinary short story one might write to a crush. There was no flowery language proclaiming my undying infatuation. No, I wrote and illustrated (yes, dear God, I illustrated it!) a story about a girl who rides off into the sunset on a giant chicken.

Seriously.

I'm hard-pressed to explain why. In fact, I can't come up with a good explanation except for the fact that I was (and am) a dork in a cheerleader's body. I look the part of someone who should be able to talk to the opposite sex, I can be animated and funny, but inside I'm a dweeb.

I asked Greg to meet me, sight unseen (at this point he couldn't possibly have known who I was), outside Ballantine Hall, where I had a late class on Thursdays. I gave him no way to contact me (because surely giving him my phone number would be far too forward—but inviting him on a blind date via a giant chicken story was perfectly reasonable?). I had to make it through class that night without underarm sweat rings forming on my shirt while I contemplated quitting school right then and joining the Peace Corps rather than face certain rejection. When eight o'clock rolled around, I stalled in the bathroom, fretting over how I looked, but the grinding in the pit of my stomach spurred me on. I was scared, appropriately so, and that's why I had to hop to it. I went skipping down the long stone staircase of Ballantine, giddy, nauseous and ready for whatever happened. If he didn't show, no one would know that I had been rejected. But there on the sidewalk, beneath a streetlamp, was Greg.

This is what I remember. He did a double take. He glanced at me, then looked again with relief, probably that I wasn't an obvious devil worshiper. Then he smiled and this was good. To the love-lorn, the mere fact that the object of a crush doesn't find you repul-sive is nothing short of inspiration to keep on keeping on. Looking back, I almost feel sorry for that guy under the streetlamp. There was nothing he could have done to discourage me short of vomit-ing on my feet in revulsion. And I also think, *Good for him!* He was game for something out of the blue and potentially strange. He showed up. And this proved to me that he was the spontaneous, fun guy I was looking for.

Now as I check my email in-box, waiting for his reply, I won-der if he's still spontaneous, still up for a slightly weird request. Will he show up again? (And, yes, I see the glaring parallel here between this and my actions in college.)

Turns out, he is. He writes back, "I do remember you, and the 'crush,' and I'd be happy to give you my account."

Reading his email, I get a jolt of excitement followed by appre-hension. Is it a good thing or bad thing that he remembers me? And why the quote marks around the word *crush?*

For our date in college, I planned something concrete so we wouldn't be forced to make small talk, which I found so painful. I knew the key code to the pottery studio in our student union, so I suggested we go there and throw some pots together. Alone in the studio, we put on white canvas aprons and got our blobs of clay. I showed him how to use the electric kick wheel and we began happily spinning lopsided pots and talking easily. Maybe that was all I needed. A forum, an activity, something to take my mind off the socially acceptable methods of flirting. I liked talking to him. He was politically informed, opinionated and fun. He was also too cool to tie the strings on his apron, which flapped around at his sides while he molded the clay with his hands.

Although I know I enjoyed being with him, in truth, I don't remember much about his personality. Or what we talked about. His appearance was probably 90 percent of the driving force behind my initial infatuation with him. Later it was what he had been writing in the newspaper that rekindled my interest. But, really I'd created my own Greg in my mind. One who was the antithesis of the guys I'd known in the small town where I grew up and different than anyone else I had dated in college. Never mind that this had little to do with who he might have been. I'd placed all my hopes and ambitions for a boyfriend onto this person as if he were a lump of clay who I could mold to my liking.

My pot was taking shape, so I focused less on my conversation with Greg, only glancing at him every now and again. The motor kept the platform spinning as I drew up the sides of the clay. I asked him a question, and when he didn't respond, I looked up to find him in mortal combat with his wheel. A loose apron string had twisted around the shaft between the platform and the kick wheel. The motor wound him closer and closer to the platform as he struggled, red-faced, to free himself from being strangled. I sat, stunned and motionless, my hands covered in clay. Then the neck strap of his apron snapped and he flew off his stool, across the room, and landed in a heap on the floor.

I gasped. He sat up, shook his head and rubbed his neck. When I saw that he was all right, I lost it. I hunched over my pottery wheel and I laughed so hard that I couldn't catch my breath and tears came to my eyes. I hunched over my pottery wheel and howled like a wild hyena over a broken-legged gazelle. Real nice. To his credit, he was a good sport about it. He tried to laugh it off, but obviously it hurt.

After we left the pottery studio, he walked me back to my apartment. It was a lovely fall evening with just enough chill in the air to promise cozy winter nights to come. I was happy. After pining away for this guy half my freshman year and then getting up the gumption to ask him out years later, I was sure things had gone well between us. Ha! Take that, love gods. I was in control of my own romantic destiny. When we got to my door, I lingered, I stalled, I flipped my hair, cracked jokes, and did everything I could think of, except grabbing his face, to show him that I was ready to kiss him. But, alas, short of donning a full body hazmat suit, he couldn't have made it more clear that nothing was going to happen between us. As he left, I wondered if it was because the pottery wheel nearly killed him and I, being a jackass, giggled about it, on and off, for the rest of the evening.

This story about my crush on Greg and our blind date gone wrong has been part of my repertoire since college, but apparently I'd forgotten a few details. When I get Greg's account of our date, his version is different than mine. He remembers me only from our senior year, when I responded to his columns in the *Indiana Daily Student,* specifically this: "I wrote a slightly fantastical conversation with Ronald McDonald about the McDonald's policy of defending foam clamshell packaging when others were ditching it. You created an illustrated booklet based on the column."

*Oh dear God,* I think with deep mortification. I sent him something else? I rack my brain. It certainly sounds like something I would do. Then from the depths of my cloudy memory, I realize he's right. I did. I made an illustrated children's book out of his column and sent it to him. I think it predated the chicken story (which he doesn't remember) but that means I sent him at least two things before I asked him out.

What the hell was wrong with me?

He goes on to say, "As I recall, [the illustrated booklet] was really well done, and I was impressed. I still have it in a box somewhere. It was the ultimate form of flattery.... It also freaked me out a bit—the rational part of me, anyway."

Despite all this, I can't help but wonder why he would have agreed to meet me. He explains it this way: "I agreed not because I was interested in or hopeful of forming some kind of romantic bond. At that stage in my life…the idea of meeting and becoming involved with someone in Indiana, which I wanted to leave as quickly as possible, was very far from my mind.... But I like people, particularly creative ones, and so I thought there'd be no harm in meeting you."

And here our impressions of our one date converge for a moment. He says, "My memory of the evening we spent together is fully positive.... I remember easy conversation. It wasn't awkward, and I was relieved, because let's face it, based on what I knew about you—you contacted me out of the blue and, never having met me, spent a lot of time and energy to communicate with me—it had the potential to be dreadful. I liked you and felt comfortable. The pottery wheel…oh yeah! I had forgotten. That's hilarious."

*How odd*, I think. He's (literally) hung on to my Ronald McDonald book, which had slipped my mind, but when I remember him, it's all about the giant chicken story and the murderous pottery wheel, which he doesn't recall. What else, I wonder, is different in the stories we tell about one another? Something significant, it turns out.

Greg writes, "After we parted that night, that was it for me until you showed up late one night on the front lawn of my house. It was raining. In my memory, there were thunderstorms. That encounter—and I can't even remember if we spoke—cast a slightly sinister glow on the whole thing for me. You had found out where I lived, pre-internet, and something was driving you to track me down in the middle of an ugly night. I started to see the Ronald McDonald booklet in a whole new light. Now it wasn't creative and flattering. It was a bit creepy. I started to attribute hang-up phone calls to you, rightly or wrongly. You became a stalker."

Oh. Dear. God. My stomach curdles and my heart drops when I read this. All these years, I've told this story as a lighthearted farce. All the while he's been spinning a parallel story of me as his college days' stalker. But he's right. I did show up at his house one night months after we'd gone out. Only, as is inevitable, my side of the story is different than his.

By this time the first Iraq war had started. Being a natural-born bleeding-heart liberal who happened to grow up in a small, conservative Midwestern town, I struggled to make sense of my feelings about the war. With the intensity only political dissidents and middle-class college students with nothing better to do can muster, I decided that the war was wrong and I should do something about it. Except I didn't know what. I took a walk that night to think this through. In my memory, I legitimately knew where Greg lived and I sought him out to talk to him about the war. He'd been writing about it in the paper and I considered him a thoughtful, informed person. I clearly remember sitting on Greg's front porch, talking about the war. He told me if there was a draft, he would take off for Mexico because the war was a sham. I thought this was dreamy, but still, I could tell he had no interest in me and was ready for me to leave.

Now I think, the poor dude was freaked out. In his mind I'd been skulking around under his window, backlit by lightning, while thunder rumbled in the distance, as if I was some freaky Stephen

KMYUEJXBEUKWBWK

King character out to lure him into my love-slave lair. Now I see why the word *crush* was in quotes in his first email to me.

I quickly emailed him back, gushing with mortification and explanation.

To Greg's credit, he says, "Forgive me if for years I have told the story of my college days' stalker. It is a story I tell for my own ego. Only cool, compelling people have stalkers. Had you not appeared that night in the rain, I would have only a memory of someone who was drawn to me by my writing, which is probably untrue, and an interesting artifact of that attraction." And he points out that "the discrepancies in our points of view make a great study of how people create tailored realities in their minds based on very little information—about other people, their intentions, how they feel."

So if you're looking for the Hollywood ending here, the one in which Uncle Greg and I reunite after twenty years and finally recognize a deep bond between us, you're reading the wrong story. My infatuation with him began to fade shortly after our one date, although I'm sure when I saw him around, I smiled and waved and maybe even had those sad puppy-dog eyes of the rejected. The last time I remember seeing him was one day in the late spring, shortly before we graduated. The weather was warm enough for everyone to be in Dunn Meadow in shorts and summer dresses. Greg walked by. He gave me that cocky flash of a smile that used to make my heart flutter and I remember thinking, did he really believe I'd pine away for him indefinitely if he wasn't interested in me? In retrospect I think, why wouldn't he have thought this? All he knew about me was that I was obsessed enough to ask him out in a bizarre way.

What I understand now is that I was the girl on the chicken. I wanted to ride into the sunset doing something ridiculous and was looking for someone to jump on with me. I hoped Greg would be that person, but in the end he was as much a figment of my imagination as I've been of his the past twenty years. I'm no more a stalker than he was the guy of my dreams. We created realities about each other that worked for us at the time, which in the end is what 99 percent of crushes turn out to be.

And so when he walked by me and smiled that last time, I smirked at him and rolled my eyes to say, "As if..." Then, I got on my giant chicken and I rode off into the sunset, looking for my next heartthrob.

# Giving Up the Ghost

## Melissa Febos

Most relationships after a certain age begin with a body or two under the bed. Usually these are ex-lovers, whose legacies manifest tangibly in shoe boxes of old letters and photos, those morbid and sentimental curations that pulse faintly from the closet shelf. Or maybe they are the specters of bad parenting, grade school bullies, criminal records, actual deaths, and surely, in some rare cases, actual cadavers. In my case, it took the form of a garbage bag full of S and M equipment.

I hadn't been retired long from the "dungeon" when I met my last boyfriend. We had actually been introduced by a former client of mine, also his best friend from college. On our first date, my skeletons were nowhere near the closet, but perched, rather, on the table between our plates of soy chicken and blanched greens. He knew before we met that in addition to having a hearty collection of exes, I had been a sex worker, a heroin addict, and that

I was writer—an occupation loath to let sleeping ghosts lie. I had already begun building the Frankenstein of my checkered past: a memoir based on my vanquished habits of spanking men and shooting dope. As a man with possessive tendencies, he should have known what he was getting himself into. But love makes us stupid, and we were no exception.

Also, I may have had a worrisome past, but my present practically defied its existence. His girlfriend was a college professor who hid her tattoos under pearl-buttoned cardigans, who went to bed at 10:00 p.m. and hadn't had even a cocktail in years. The door to my former life seemed firmly closed, and so, three months into our relationship, the door to our new apartment opened. I left my loft in the hipster ghetto of Williamsburg and moved to the leafy haven of Prospect Heights, where there were more baby strollers than bars, and prepared to enter the next level of domestication.

And then the paddle slipped out from under the bed. It was black, the length of an arm, and outfitted with a strip of sandpaper on one side. I found him standing over it one afternoon, brow furrowed.

"Um. Do I want to know what that's for?"

"Probably not." I laughed and kicked it back under the bed, hoping my nonchalance was contagious. He stared at the floor where the paddle had been, and then up at me. I scrambled to think of something to distract him from whatever it was he wanted to say.

"You planning on using that again anytime soon?" He smiled halfway and cocked an eyebrow.

"Of course not! I just need to get around to selling it." I reached across the bed to the window and turned up the air conditioner. He was still looking at me when I finished, so I grabbed a stray T-shirt and began folding it. "You know, what I really need to do is get on eBay." I didn't look up again until I felt his gaze move away from me.

The paddle wasn't alone. Its sharp edges had simply chewed a hole in the black garbage bag that housed a wide assortment of similar artifacts. Leather cuffs, corsets, rubber (disinfected!) enema bags and platform stilettos nestled into a cocoon of latex catsuits, nurse uniforms and pleated miniskirts I was pretty sure I'd crossed the outer age bracket of eligibility for. When I had hung my floggers up for good, and cleaned out my locker in the dungeon dressing room, I had shoved it all—thousands of dollars' worth of equipment and costumery—into the industrial-strength bag. The bag had sat under my bed in Williamsburg for months, and then among the last of my boxes as I'd moved, its fate uncertain. As I'd stood over it in those final moments, the pang I'd felt—something between the feeling of throwing a birthday card from your grandmother in the trash and just before you answer a phone call from someone you know will probably break your heart—was too strong to override. The body in that bag was still too warm. I rationalized that the contents of the bag were worth too much money, and carried it to the moving van.

A month after the paddle incident, a red leather riding crop wandered out from under the dust ruffle. My boyfriend was at work this time, and I got down on my knees and tugged the lumpy mass out from under our bed. When I unknotted the bag's neck, it exhaled a ghostly breath: the scent of stale incense, body sweat, leather, my old perfume (Dior's Addict) and rubbing alcohol. My heart and stomach lurched in unison. It was the smell of the dungeon, the smell of my past, the smell of desire and money, of secrecy and sex. It was the olfactory equivalent of an old mix tape: a sensory time capsule.

I reasoned that the memoir ought to have presented a graver threat of the past's reincarnation. But my writing happened in silence; it didn't have a smell. Reliving the past in writing was intense, but also left the memories flattened somewhat, defanged. I know that the potential rise of that Frankenstein, though it gave my partner pangs of his own, seemed at that point mostly hypothetical. The act of writing down a story places it firmly in the past, draws a line between then and now, the story and its telling. So long as my alter identity—Mistress Justine—and her interest in the business of desire stayed on the far side of that line, he could see her as evidence of my depth; she was enough to render me exotic, but not too dangerous.

But the objects in that bag did have a smell. Their presence was a tangible reminder of my reluctance to let them go. I knew they would only get louder; their smell more pungent. And I felt his wariness—a texture in the air between us that hadn't been there before, as he must have felt that body under the bed go bump in the night while I slept.

I didn't keep the bag around for its monetary value, true, but the straight life *was* cash poor. I knew it was time to unload the past, but I wasn't so dramatic that I needed to burn it in effigy. Sifting through the contents of that bag, half in inventory, half in nostalgia, I thought of the iSold It on eBay store on Flatbush Avenue, a few blocks west of our apartment. I'd noticed it the day we moved in, was reminded of Catherine Keener in *The 40-Year-Old Virgin,* and had since nurtured a warm association to the bland storefront.

So, after a thorough wipe down with said rubbing alcohol, I loaded the corsets, heels, leather goods and nurse uniforms into a compact wheeling suitcase. The latex, dildos, clamps, gags and rope I left in the garbage bag, reknotting the neck. I dragged both down the apartment stairs, and as I passed the garbage can on the corner of our block, I unceremoniously dropped the bag into it. The pang I felt this time was manageable.

It was summer, not sweltering yet, but enough that after four blocks in jeans, pulling the suitcase as it bumped cheerfully over every crack and pebble, I boasted sweat stains and a shiny forehead when I arrived at the door of the iSold It on eBay store. I had spent the walk awash in memories of my old life, the exhilaration and shame that I'd felt each day, going to a job that paid me in cash and desire. For what? What had I been selling then? My body, fantasies, my own deep-seated need to be desired. As fantasies always had, the ones I traded at the dungeon had allowed me to lose myself, and they'd forced me to. The symbolism of this imminent act wasn't lost on me. I was selling my disguises, the freedom they afforded, and the alienation they inflicted. Regardless, it hadn't dawned on me how public an act it was going to be. When I entered the air-conditioned cool of the store, my sweat turned cold as I beheld the small crowd inside. Building a secret life almost always happens in private, but eschewing one, it seems, never can.

I joined a short line of waiting customers and watched as they were each delegated to an iSold It employee. The sellers plopped their unwanted valuables on the long sales counter and the employees examined them. The iSold It employees performed searches on eBay for similar items and then affixed tags with a comparable price to the objects in question, to be posted live at a later time. As I moved closer to the counter, my palm slipped on the suitcase's handle. I wiped both hands on my jeans and cleared my throat, watching the door for other hopeful sellers. *Dear God,* I thought, *I know I must be some kind of exhibitionist, but let there not be an audience for this.* Two of the employees were men, youngish, not ostensibly the type to have encountered the sort of contents my suitcase held. But then, I knew better than anyone the misleading superficiality of covers, especially the kind to those sorts of books. Nonetheless, I prayed to be assigned the woman employee, who looked like the kind of bland, hearty stock that could at least affect a nonchalant disposition. She wore pleated chinos and had a face like uncooked poultry. Hoisting a complicated-looking baby knapsack over the countertop, she smiled earnestly at the man in front of me. Nice, she looked really nice. Not at all like the type to try and trade her services for spankings, like a personal trainer to whom I'd once made the mistake of divulging my work. I desperately hoped she was nice, as sturdy as her body looked. Perhaps in the narcissism of my own fear I was like a child petrified of a honey bee—oblivious to the outlandish threat of my own size. A different person would have been worried for her, I suppose.

It only occurs to me now that I might have been seeking such a thrill. One of the principle pleasures of being a dominatrix had been the shock I could elicit from almost anyone. In my book, I'd already admitted my lifelong fascination with "the ability to appear one thing, and to be another." I had always sought to embody polarities—high school dropout with a graduate degree, marathon-training smoker, summa cum laude heroin junkie—because they not only empowered me to defy social prescription, but also upset just about anyone's expectations. I loved the look of shock on people's faces when I told them I was a dominatrix. Because *I* was nice. I didn't hate men. I could have gotten real jobs if I'd wanted to. I was a sex worker by choice, not out of desperation. The high of exercising that power was part of what I dreaded surrendering. But I didn't feel empowered as I stood in the iSold It store in my girl-next-door outfit with my suitcase full of domme gear. I felt quietly horrified. There is a high in horror, I know, as a former junkie and sex worker. But if there was pleasure in that moment, I sure didn't feel it.

I got the woman.

"Hi there!" she chirruped. "And what do you have for me today?"

I just smiled back to the best of my ability and hoisted the suitcase onto the counter between us. She tilted her head to the side, waiting for some further introduction. I knew there was nothing for me to say and so I let the silence swell between us until she finally gave a little "N'kay," still cheerful, and unzipped the suitcase. She opened it and stared inside for perhaps only a few beats longer than if it had held a collection of doilies. I surveyed her surveying my old bondage equipment and didn't take a breath until she raised her gaze to mine and mercifully suggested that we "take this to the computer in the back, where there is a little more room." Her tone in that moment may have contained a note of humor, but it was so subtle that I didn't dare to respond except to say that "yes, a little more room might be nice." Though we spent the next thirty minutes head to head, poring through the trappings of my old persona, she went no further to acknowledge the remarkability of my wares. Not that I wasn't grateful for the gesture. It broke my heart a little, in that sweet way, her effort to circumvent both our embarrassment.

"And what would you call these?" she asked me, pulling the leather, fur-lined cuffs from the suitcase.

"Cuffs? No, leather restraints."

"N'kay. Leather restraints," she repeated in her pragmatic voice, typing the words in the search window. Together we watched similar images appear on the screen. I could feel the warmth of her shoulder, inches away from my own, smell her clean, powdery scent. And so on with the stilettos, riding crop, paddle and uniforms. I didn't have the heart to argue when she vastly underpriced the value of my favorite corset.

Leaving the iSold It store with my empty suitcase was like waking from a dream, not a nightmare, but one I was glad to wake from, nonetheless. The garbage bag with my dildos in it was still at the bottom of the can on the corner when I passed by on my way home.

My boyfriend was unmistakably relieved when I told him I'd sold the body under the bed. The checks arrived by mail over the next few weeks, a small fraction of what I knew my past was worth. I wasn't done, of course. I let go of that life, yes, but not the story. I couldn't lay that body to rest until I'd learned how it ended. The book sold a year later, and not to an anonymous buyer on eBay, whom we'd never have to face. That relationship didn't survive in the end, not my history, and everything else that weighs on love, and more heavily as it thins over time. There wasn't enough room in our home for both my story and ours, and we never managed to fit them together into one narrative. Now he haunts me, and surely my new love wishes his phantom gone, as I do hers.

Of course, it is we who are most haunted by our own histories, who absently run our fingers over old scars, our gaze drifting out windows at the familiar notes of old songs and the scent of sweatshirts pulled out of storage. But it is also the living inhabitants of our lives who suffer their presence. Who hasn't nurtured the private exhaustion of loving patience, and wished for the exorcism of our lover's ex-lovers? Our lover's former lives? We want our loves to ourselves; we want to occupy the parts of them that belong to other people, other places, things that cannot be exiled because they are already gone. We harbor this desire out of selfishness, but ultimately, perhaps out of fear. The most considerate partners try to keep these corpses out of sight, behind the dust bunnies and unused workout equipment, or even better, finally lugged out with the objects we keep out of sentiment. I haven't always been this kind of partner, but I have tried. And I'm not sorry to be haunted by my ghosts. They guide me from one life to the next. But I am not sorry to let them go, either.

# What Kitty Taught Me
## Christopher Coake

I think and talk about first love these days more than I ever supposed I would back when I had yet to experience it. I teach fiction writing at a university, and at least once a semester a student will turn in a story steeped in the remembered agony of first love. This is inevitable; the majority of my students have only just become adults and/or are entering into the first serious relationships that give them—at last—the perspective they've needed in order to understand the loneliness that, surely, afflicted them as adolescents.

(I hate to stereotype, but come on: if creative writers had been less lonely in junior high, would they ever have had time to learn to write?)

I do not exclude myself. During my sophomore year of high school I wrote a novel about a young man who a) could perform miracles, and b) was admired, and often pleasured, by women he encountered, because of his awesome creative energies, his under-lying sensitivity.

But would I have traded every word of that novel, the hundreds of hours of its making, for a girlfriend? Did I show that novel to bookish girls I liked, hoping one of them would be so impressed by the hidden truths therein as to *become* my girlfriend?

What do you think?

What I mean to say is that dispensing wisdom about first love has become an unexpected subspecialty of mine. The result is that when my class workshops such a first-love story, I tend to roll out a stock speech—something about how paradoxical it is that we love most intensely when we're children; something about how our first love is, in many ways, our *purest* love, never to be duplicated.

My students are generally all polite enough to nod while I'm talking. I suspect, however, this speech more often than not appalls them. Most fiction writers are idealists, really; at some level all my students want to believe in the power of true love—that any of their loves, especially the ones that might await them, could be pure. My speech makes them search themselves; they listen and squint their eyes hard at both their pasts and their futures, as well as at their jaded professor and his inky, pessimistic heart.

The speech does, in other words, what any good fiction ought to.

I suppose I didn't realize this—that I might have been lying to them all along—until I sat down to write about my own first love. I almost never do this in nonfiction. Fiction? Sure—my stories are well stocked with sensitive romantic types, seized up by past fail-ures in love. And I mention first, failed loves all the time; this is part of my penance as a registered nerd.

When I talk about junior high and high school in front of my students (because I tend to, in order to undercut the cynicism of my first-love speech), I play up those years as comedy—I present myself as a Michael Cera-esque fool, too obsessed with Tolkien and *Dungeons and Dragons* to make anything but charmingly awkward mistakes around all those pretty, mysterious, kindhearted girls. There's some method to this; I remember being in college, still making high school mistakes in matters of love (and hardly being charming about it)—and I remember, then, perking up at the stories of married adults. I took considerable pleasure in learning not only that my professors and role models had been hopeless nerds, too, but that they'd *survived*—that an accomplished adulthood could, in time, transform the pain of childhood into a good laugh.

So I tell my students lies, and I take a few pratfalls, and in the end we laugh and move on, pretending we're all wise adults. And why not? Fiction's about pretending, not only for the benefit of others, but oftentimes—most of all—for ourselves.

I have a further confession: I'm not sure who my first love even *was*. I had so many horrible, gut-wrenching crushes that choosing the primal one, the *ur*-crush, seems to depend too much on a definition of love that has eluded far better philosophers and artists than me.

My implied fiction-class definition fails me, here, especially: If I loved any of these girls *purely*—with more passion and selflessness, say, than I've ever felt since—why am I so hesitant to write any of it down? If first love is sacrosanct, why am I so reluctant to consider it?

I see now I loved none of those girls purely; that I imply I did now is due only to shame. When I was fourteen, fifteen, sixteen, I was only a creature of *want*. I ached for particular girls, sure; I lay awake at night dreaming about how one of them might finally look me in the eye and say (because, given who I was, she'd pretty much have to): "I've been lying to myself. I don't need my boyfriend the way I need you"—or one of a hundred other stock lines, almost surely less pure than those. Some of these girls were friendly to me, which meant they were nicer people than they had any call to be…but was I ever any kind of friend to them in return?

I wasn't, I'm afraid. A friend, after all, would not be a creature of want; a friend would act selflessly, at least from time to time; a friend would share information; a friend would be curious about his friend's inner life. But moony, love-struck me didn't learn this sort of stuff. It never occurred to me to want to. That boy was too busy declaring love (because whatever he was, that boy wasn't shy). That boy, if he ever imagined one of his female friends' inner lives, noted either that he was a treasured part of it, or wasn't.

He loved those girls for their *potential* love of him—but since none of them loved him, or ever came to love him, he was really loving phantoms, inventions: beings no more real than the tough, magic-wielding women who loved his novel's protagonist, who told him exactly what he wanted to hear, for page after page after page, almost as though he'd conjured them from the air for that purpose alone.

Which brings me, in a roundabout way, to the subject of this essay. The more I consider young and foolish me, the more I think it's most appropriate to tell you about the strangest and most irrational of my childhood loves. The only one who, in retrospect, I might have loved *purely*.

We were never friends, she and I; she never knew me, and will never know me. I became aware of her around my freshman year of high school, when a couple of nerdy friends of mine pointed her out to me, and right away I saw her as special: someone very lovable indeed.

Her name was Katherine "Kitty" Pryde—aka Shadowcat, a member of the X-Men.

You think I'm joking. Looking at my fears and insecurities and punting the essay into comedy.

This is love we're talking about. Trust me when I say I don't think it's funny at all.


As an adolescent I had an insatiable appetite for fantasy narrative. I got into comics for the same reason a lot of kids do; I was a powerless loser, and the comics were full of powerful outcasts, and yadda, yadda, yadda—that's an old idea, and I was as susceptible to it as any other spindly, be-zitted boy who ever felt moved to buy a Wolverine T-shirt and wear it to dances. I was a Marvel guy; I loved the Fantastic Four, I loved Spider Man and the Hulk. I loved the X-Men—the most outcast of heroes—above all the others.

Kitty Pryde was, at about the time I was reading, one of the newest members of the X-Men. She was the youngest of the team: a teenaged girl, awkward but whip-smart, unsure of herself in many ways, but brave when it counted. As Shadowcat, Kitty Pryde could make herself insubstantial—she could slip through walls and floors; she could even hide inside people. For a long time she was unsure if this ability was even powerful enough to be useful. She wasn't just a mutant, either; Kitty was *Jewish*—and where I grew up, out in the Indiana cornfields, that qualified her as damned exotic. Everyone on the team loved Kitty, but she spent a lot of time hanging out with Wolverine—the coolest comic hero of all time, bar none—who gave her life lessons and looked out for her, and in so doing transmitted much of his cool to her. Kitty had a boyfriend, a Russian X-Man named Colossus, but it was apparent to me that they were a bad match (Colossus wasn't that deep); sure enough, they didn't last long.

Kitty had a pet dragon, for Chrissakes, about the size of a dachshund. Kitty was awesome.

My old comics are long gone, but I remember clearly the way various artists (especially John Byrne, Kitty's creator) drew her in her formfitting costume—gawky, skinny and appalled, like she wanted to cover herself with her arms. Her curly brown hair spilled out from beneath her mask, as though by accident. Her eyes, behind that mask, seemed way too big.

She was pretty, yes, but the comics were clear that she was still a child: unfinished and a little fragile-seeming, despite her bravery. Whenever the X-Men went into battle, I worried for Kitty; my heart would pound for her.

When she was safe—when the battle was over, but before she found her way into Colossus's arms—I was exultant.

Superhero comics were and still are largely written by men. Young me was aware that Kitty Pryde was a creation of a man (John Byrne, in this case, whom I idolized); I was aware that a man drew her, inked the lines, colored her in, carefully transcribed each letter of every one of her words. If Kitty ever said something that seemed to speak directly to the soul of an adolescent boy—and she often did—well, that was likely by design; I was aware of this. Kitty Pryde wasn't real, couldn't be real—I never thought otherwise.

For all these reasons I didn't, couldn't, feel lust for Kitty—not in the chaotic, suffocating way I felt lust out in the world, when the rustle of a girl's clothes at the locker next to mine could make me dizzy. Sure, Kitty was beautiful; if she *had* been real, and had had the locker next to mine, I'm sure she would have made my palms sweat. But because some tubby fellow had drawn her, because another put words into her mouth, because I wasn't insane—I stress this—I didn't *have* lust for Kitty.

And this lack of lust was a relief. While reading *The X-Men*, I didn't have to worry—for once!—about the reactions of my body. And without having to worry about Kitty's body, and what it did or did not do to mine, I was free to focus on Kitty's character.

Kitty had been written by several different authors over a series of years; that meant her words and her past were deep and complex and searchable. In any single frame of a comic in which she appeared, Kitty was beautiful, yes. But Kitty's *mind*—her hopes and dreams and fears—was much greater than any image of her. The totality of her was accessible only to someone dedicated. Faithful.

And that was me. I was faithful to Kitty, to her history and growth. Either by spending my allowance or borrowing titles from friends, I managed, over the course of a year, to read just about every comic she appeared in. I listened to her, and paid heed, without any hope of consummation. In this small, sad way, I pledged my troth.

Doesn't that sound like love?

Maybe. Maybe not. It's not like I knew what I was doing then; I wasn't aware of what I was learning. *She's in a damn comic book, you dolt,* I used to think. *You're hopeless.*

I didn't truly fall in love with someone *real* until my twenties. Even when I went to college and had actual girlfriends, and employed the word *love*, and heard it employed, I hadn't yet lost the bad habits of my adolescence. I depended on melodramatic declarations and adoration. I still felt, even after a simple kiss, that I was owed something magical and special and consuming and lusty, and that belief got me nowhere fast.

It wasn't until I was a graduate student at Miami University of Ohio, and met the woman who would someday become my first wife, that I understood at last what a character in a damn *comic book* had once demonstrated.

That real woman—my office mate, a graduate student in rhetoric and composition named Joellen Thomas—was diagnosed with cancer shortly after we met. Thereafter Joellen had to leave school; her physical self (which I liked a great deal, which had kissed me one night, and had made me a creature of want) was suddenly gone from the office we shared, and for a year she and I could only talk on the telephone. Her cancer kept her physical self uncertain; I saw soon enough that if I was to love Joellen, and she me, then— in this absence of a possible future—we might *have* to rely on the untouchable: Our pasts, our voices. Our stories.

And in this way—slowly, surely, through long telephone calls and letters and emails—we did come to love one another, deeply. We reunited when it was possible; for a time we lived together; for a time we were married.

Joellen died in 1999. The cancer that she'd fought so bravely, after a period of remission lasting almost a year, came back for her only a few months after our wedding. Before our first anniversary she was gone.

I keep coming back to the lie I've told my students. What do I mean by it?

My first "loves" weren't pure. My love for Kitty Pryde was pure enough, but she was not real.

My love for my first wife—wasn't *that* pure? Maybe. As a couple we were not without our flaws. Joellen would be the last person on earth to insist that her sickness made either of us better people, or our romance more sanctified than someone else's. But I loved her mightily all the same.

Furthermore, to say any of these loves was pure—more pure than any other—discounts my present. I'm remarried now; in 2002 I met Stephanie Lauer, and nearly a decade later, she is still with me. We fell for each other in the right way—the way I learned from my junior high crushes, from Kitty, from Joellen. On our first date we talked for hours and hours. I expected nothing except the possible delight in another's company; I kept interest ahead of want. Now we live in a small house on the edge of the desert with two boisterous dogs. To what would certainly have been the shock of any number of my past selves—not least of them the man who watched Joellen die—I consider myself a happy man. Lucky in love.

The word *pure,* as applied to an emotion, is worse than a fiction. It's a dream.

More and more it's clear that I err in pretending to know anything about love at all. I know everything and nothing. Some of my students have never been kissed; some are divorced; others are married and pregnant. All of us in the workshop room write because we are obsessed with this complexity—we can no more reduce love to a line than we can death, the terrible consequences of mutant genes, the Power Cosmic.

Maybe I lie because I'm old enough, now, to see as much in my past as in my possible future. To see my body start to give way. To wish for *the way things were.* In all respects I am balanced in the middle of a life, between spans of years, between two different visions of happiness. Complexity comes at a cost. I yearn, maybe, for a first love even more primal and odd and weird than that I felt for Kitty.

Maybe my first love was for purity itself. For something awesome and whole, something without stain, something as unreal as a drawing on a page, as immortal.

Like most people who read them, I grew out of my comics, with surprising speed; by my junior year I had quit collecting and was back to imagining my way into novels and preparing for college.

For several years in my twenties I worked in a used bookstore. I often spent my lunch breaks flipping through the stacks of old comics we sometimes sold; in this way I found out a little of what happened to Kitty—she'd left the X-Men and moved to England; she'd had her heart broken more than once. She'd become an adult, more or less as I had, and seemed no worse for our separation. Neither did I.

This is not to say I don't miss her. I do.

Even now, in my late thirties, I walk into comic book shops—for old times' sake; I'm powerless not to—and open old issues of *The X-Men*. Seeing Kitty there, I feel a shock, as though I've run into an old flame in line at the bank.

Sometimes, in the dusty back corners of these shops, an old comic slipped carefully out of its longbox and sleeve, Kitty in front of me, I allow myself—for a few seconds—to be transported. I can summon up—effortlessly—the old thrill of buying a new month's comic or a back issue. I remember the thrill of discovering some part of Kitty's story I did not know; of lying on my bed, the world around me vanishing as I flipped the pages, until at last I failed to see them as pages at all, until I seemed to be a student, too, at Xavier's school. I recall the yearning—not for flesh, not really, but for something much more complex: for the ability to reach out my hand *into* the images in front of me; to make the unreal real.

I remembered the sadness, too, that inevitable sadness that always came when these desires I reached for—like Kitty herself—revealed themselves as phantoms, and slipped away.

We are lucky to love at all, I will tell my students the next time. I will tell them that a first love can be as valuable as our last.

I will tell them that some loves we can measure only through the magnitude of their loss.

# Before It Gets Complicated

## Rebecca Woolf

She runs to the slide and Archer's eyes follow. He stands still for a moment, waiting for her signal to come join her at the ladder. Instead she climbs, lifts her hands and swirls down the twists by herself. And then she does it again and again—up she climbs and down she goes and Archer continues watching until he becomes self-conscious and turns back toward me. I'm watching him and he knows it, gives me a look like, "Stop looking at me, Mom. You're distracting me with the loudness of your thoughts."

I have a tendency to do that, think so hard that Archer has to cover his ears.

I rock my newborn daughter in my arms and blink sideways, spying through my sunglasses as Archer casually makes his way toward his friend. He looks back at me to make sure I'm not watching until finally he forgets I'm behind him and stops looking back.

♥♥♥

All my friends used to be boys. When you're a small child, it doesn't matter who's carrying what equipment. Lines need not be drawn in the sand. Bathrooms are unisex and so are ideas. There is no pressure to maintain relationships. No fear of when they might end. No girlfriends or boyfriends or sex, just the occasional hand-holding under the swings.

Marriage changes that. The fairy tale has taught us that true love means never having to lust after anyone else, let alone seek companionship outside of our relationships. Monogamy is a religion we are taught to praise and respect for its all-knowing power. "I only have eyes for you," we say in so many words as we exchange rings and bodily fluids. But is it true? Does it have to be true? And what of the innocence of crushes—of the fantasy, sexual or not, of lying with someone else, brushing hands with a stranger in an elevator and feeling, for a moment, the warmth of unknown possibilities?

I have always believed in one true love but also in a thousand true likes. I only have eyes for everybody in the room so long as I remember not to stare.... *It's rude to stare....*

And yet...

Last year I met a guy at a bar. Harmless flirting ensued over cocktails and cigarettes on the patio. He asked me my name and in return gave me his.

"Rebecca."

"Andrew."

"Nice to meet you."

"Same."

He asked me where I was from and in turn told me his story. He had recently graduated from college and moved west to pursue film and music. He had a band. He casually mentioned his childhood in New Jersey. The small town he grew up in outside of Princeton, where his father was a professor. The story became familiar. The name of the town. His last name. Until... "Wait. What did you say your last name was, again? What was the name of that town? Oh my God. I *know* you. I *knew* you."

I had heard his name a hundred times, seen his face in various photo albums as my parents reminisced about the two years they had lived in New Jersey, where I was born. Our fathers worked together and our mothers were best friends. Twenty-six years ago, we were best friends.

"Your name," I said, "was my first word. Your name!"

The world was suddenly pea-size and we were clutching it together, slurring our mutual words of disbelief.

I jumped up and down, shrieking, and he just laughed. He laughed and then I laughed and then he called his mother, who was asleep, and I called my mother, who was dreaming, and we linked arms and spoke so fast it was impossible to understand what we were saying.

"Mom! You will never believe who I ran intoyouwon'tbelieveit momthisissocrazydidIwakeyouup..."

Once the initial excitement wore off, we sat down at the bar and just sort of stared at each other.

Attracted to each other by fate or familiarity, we spent the remainder of the evening trying to catch up, a friendship that never made it past the dawn of our lives.... What if I never moved away? I kept thinking. Would our friendship have lasted into the afternoon?

When I found out I was unexpectedly pregnant with Archer, I had known his father, my husband, for only three months. It showed. I removed my wedding ring many a night those first few years of marriage so that I could meet boys like Andrew and fib to their faces about who I was. Pretending for an evening out that I wasn't married or a mother or *me*.

Flirting and crushing and collecting free drinks, bumming cigarettes I knew I shouldn't smoke, huffing the shirts of strangers to catch a buzz, I told tales too tall to reach in platform booties, satiating my own need for rebellion through lipstick-stained lies.

I resented Hal in the beginning of our marriage because I thought he wanted to keep me from my life—to take away my open road and replace it with a cul-de-sac. No outlet. I resented him far more than I resented Archer for making me a mother. *Being a wife was the reason I felt so alone.*

But my loneliness, it seemed, was a construct of my own fear. One day I spoke up and everything changed. I had been wrong to feel trapped. I was in nobody's cage but my own. A cage I had likely spent my life and every serious relationship building and breaking down, afraid I might fall under someone's spell.

I watch Archer and think back on the night, well over a year ago, when I reunited with Andrew. How we exchanged phone numbers and promised to get together. Meet for drinks. Dinner. I promised to come out and see his band play. We swore we'd absolutely remain friends because what were the chances of old friends from New Jersey meeting at a bar in downtown Los Angeles twenty-six years later? Unable to recognize one another because we were babies when I moved away? It had to have been a sign of some kind. Or perhaps, as it so often does, it meant nothing.

Andrew and I texted each other several times. Made plans that fell through. Never saw each other again.

It's complicated now. Too complicated, perhaps, to re-friend a man who used to be a boy I bathed naked with in my mother's garden. Because no matter how many marital stereotypes I rebel against publicly, I'm a mother and a wife and I shouldn't discount that. I don't want to discount that.

Still, I miss Andrew. I miss the way we met as children and the way we reunited as adults: old friends, now strangers, with promises to meet again. I miss the way life felt barefoot and uncomplicated, before my thoughts were loud enough to hear from the farthest end of the sandbox.

Maybe we'll run into each other again, I think as I watch Archer chase my friend's daughter through a vacant swing set. *Maybe we'll meet at a different dimly lit bar and I'll offer to buy him a drink....*

I often think about friends who fell out of touch—the boy friends that were never boyfriends. Our adventures on skateboards. Our trips to the desert, bunched up in the passenger seats of beat-up trucks. Poop jokes and takeout and smoking cigarettes out of bedroom windows. Trading mix tapes and quoting movies and drinking out of each other's plastic cups.

It changes when you get married. As the years pass by, platonic relationships become impossibly complicated. Risk becomes more than reward. Meetings begin and then end within moments instead of over months, years. We must hold back, learn to say no. Cross our legs and our mouths and sometimes even our minds to keep from falling. Because we're adults and we know too much. Because we're human and danger is our middle name.

So many times I've had to look away in order to focus on what's truly important—wholeheartedly happy here, *now,* feet in the sand, watching Archer experiment with his *Andrew*s as I let go of fading photographs to make way for digital cameras.

I may have eyes for everyone in the room, but it's Hal I choose to share a table with.

I turn toward the swing set just in time to see Archer hold his friend by the hand before letting it go.

# contributors' notes

**Steve Almond** is the author of two story collections, *My Life in Heavy Metal* and *The Evil B.B. Chow*; the novel *Which Brings Me to You* (with Julianna Baggott), and the nonfiction books *Candyfreak* and *(Not That You Asked)*. His most recent book, *Rock and Roll Will Save Your Life*, came out in spring 2010. He is also, crazily, self-publishing books. *This Won't Take But a Minute, Honey*, is composed of thirty very brief stories and thirty very brief essays on the psychology and practice of writing. *Letters from People Who Hate Me* is just plumb crazy. Both are available at readings. In 2011 Lookout Press will publish his story collection *God Bless America*.

**Katherine Center** is the author of three novels about love and family—*The Bright Side of Disaster*, *Everyone Is Beautiful* and *Get Lucky*—and has more on the way. Her books and essays have appeared in *Redbook*, *People*, *USA Today*, *Vanity Fair*, *Real Simple*, the *Dallas Morning News*, and the *Houston Chronicle*, as well as the anthology *Because I Love Her: 34 Women Writers Reflect on the Mother-Daughter Bond*. Varsity Pictures optioned Katherine's first novel last fall. Katherine lives in Houston with her husband and two young children. Please see her website: www.katherinecenter.com.

**Christopher Coake** is the author of the story collection *We're in Trouble* (Harcourt, 2005), for which he was named the PEN/Robert Bingham Fellow in 2006. In 2007 he was named a Best Young American Novelist by *Granta*. His short fiction has been published in journals such as *Epoch*, the *Southern Review*, the *Gettysburg Review* and *Five Points*, and has been anthologized in *The Best American Mystery Stories 2004* and the forthcoming *The Best American Noir of the Century*. He lives with his wife and two dogs in Reno, where he teaches creative writing at the University of Nevada.

**Kerry Cohen** is the author of *Loose Girl: A Memoir of Promiscuity*, as well as three young adult novels. Two more books—*Dirty Little Secrets* and *Seeing Ezra*—are forthcoming. Her essays have been featured in the *New York Times* Modern Love series, the *Washington Post*, *Brevity* and other journals and anthologies. She lives in Portland, Oregon, with her family.

**Melissa Febos** is the author of the critically acclaimed memoir *Whip Smart* (Thomas Dunne Books/St. Martin's Press). She has been featured on NPR's *Fresh Air* with Terry Gross and the cover of the *New York Post*, among many other national publications. Her writing has been published in venues such as *Hunger Mountain*, *Dissent*, the *Southeast Review*, *Redivider*, the *Rambler*, *Storyscape Journal*, the *Huffington Post*, the *New York Times* online, *Bitch* magazine, the *Chronicle Review* and the *Nervous Breakdown*, where she regularly blogs. She co-curates and hosts the Mixer Reading and Music Series at Cake Shop; teaches at SUNY Purchase College, the Gotham Writers' Workshop, the New School and NYU. Recently named one of "Five New Queer Voices to Watch Out For" by the Lambda Literary Foundation, she is the winner of the Memoirs Ink half-yearly contest and a 2010 MacDowell Colony fellow. She lives in Brooklyn. More information about her work and projects can be found at melissafebos.com.

An international bestselling and award-winning novelist, **Suzanne Finnamore**'s books have been translated into fourteen languages. *Split: A Memoir of Divorce* was chosen as a *Library Journal* Book of the Year in 2008. She has been published in the *New York Times*, the *London Times*, the *Guardian, Salon*, NPR online, *Mademoiselle, Glamour, Marie Claire, Modern Bride* and *Redbook*; she is a frequent contributor to Oprah Winfrey's *O Magazine*. She lives in the Carolinas with her family.

**Emily Franklin** is the author of over a dozen novels for teens, including *The Half-Life of Planets* (cowritten with Brendan Halpin) and *Jenna and Jonah's Fauxmance*, as well as the critically acclaimed series *The Principles of Love*. She also writes books for adults. Visit her at emilyfranklin.com.

**Amy Greene** was born and raised in the foothills of the Smoky Mountains, where she still lives with her husband, Adam, a freelance sportswriter, and their two children, Emma and Taylor. Her first novel, *Bloodroot*, was published by Alfred A. Knopf in January 2010. Her second novel, *Long Man*, is forthcoming, also from Knopf.

**Brendan Halpin** is the author of two memoirs and four novels for adults, including the Alex Award–winning *Donorboy*. He also writes novels for young adults, including *Forever Changes, The Half-Life of Planets* (with Emily Franklin), *Shutout* and *Notes from the Blender* (with Trish Cook). Widowed at thirty-five, he developed a huge crush on a beautiful teacher at his daughter's elementary school. At thirty-six, he married her. Brendan and Suzanne live in Boston with their children Casey, Rowen and Kylie.

**Katie Herzog** has a BA in literature from the University of North Carolina–Asheville. She has been a raft guide, census worker, diamond seller, ghost writer, mascot, Christmas elf, and is currently a copy editor and freelance writer. She lives in Durham, North Carolina. Visit her blog at twentytwentyhindsight.com.

**Ann Hood** is the author of nine novels, including *Somewhere Off the Coast of Maine*, *The Knitting Circle* and, most recently, *The Red Thread*. She has also written two memoirs, *Do Not Go Gentle: My Search for Miracles in a Cynical Time* and *Comfort: A Journey Through Grief*, which was a *New York Times* Editors' Choice and one of *Entertainment Weekly*'s Top Ten Nonfiction Books of 2008. Her essays and short stories have appeared in the *New York Times*, the *Paris Review*, the *Washington Post*, *O, The Oprah Magazine*, *Glimmer Train*, *Tin House* and many other publications. The winner of two Pushcart Prizes, the Paul Bowles Prize for Short Fiction and a Best American Spiritual Writing Award, she lives in Providence, Rhode Island.

**Sheila Kohler** is the author of seven novels and three collections of stories. Her work has been anthologized in *The Best American Short Stories* and the PEN/O. Henry Prize Stories and she has won the Willa Cather Prize. Her latest novel is *Becoming Jane Eyre*, based on the life of Charlotte Brontë. Her novel *Cracks* has been filmed, with Jordan Scott and Ridley Scott as directors. Eva Green plays Miss G.

**David Levithan** is the author of many acclaimed young adult novels, including *Boy Meets Boy*, *The Realm of Possibility*, *Love Is the Higher Law* (an IndieBound Top Ten pick), *Nick & Norah's Infinite Playlist* (with Rachel Cohn), which was turned into a popular movie, and (with John Green) *Will Grayson, Will Grayson*. His latest novel, this time about grown-ups, is *The Lover's Dictionary*.

**Jacquelyn Mitchard** is the author of eighteen novels, including several *New York Times* bestsellers, among them *The Deep End of the Ocean,* the first selection of the Oprah's Book Club. A contributing editor for *Parade* magazine, she lives near Madison, Wisconsin, with her husband and their nine children.

**Joshua Mohr** is the author of the novels *Some Things that Meant the World to Me,* which was one of *O Magazine*'s Top Ten reads of 2009, and the newly released *Termite Parade.* He has an MFA from the University of San Francisco and has published numerous short stories and essays in publications such as *7×7,* the *Bay Guardian, ZYZZYVA,* the *Rumpus, Other Voices,* the *Cimarron Review, Gulf Coast* and *Pleiades,* among many others. He teaches fiction writing in San Francisco.

**Catherine Newman** is the author of the memoir *Waiting for Birdy* and writes for a lot of different magazines, including *Family Fun, O, The Oprah Magazine* and *Body + Soul.* She writes a weekly food and parenting column, "Dalai Mama Dishes," on family.com and wrote "Bringing Up Ben and Birdy" on babycenter.com. Her work has been published in lots of anthologies, including the *New York Times* bestselling *The Bitch in the House.* She lives in Amherst, where she has many crushes on people and their smells.

**Lauren Oliver's** debut novel, *Before I Fall,* was a *New York Times* bestseller and will be translated into twenty-one languages. Her novels *Delirium* and *Liesl and Po* will be forthcoming in 2011. Lauren lives in Brooklyn, New York, when she is not living out of a suitcase. Please visit her at www.laurenoliverbooks.com.

**Jon Skovron** lives with his two sons outside Washington, D.C. His first novel, *Struts & Frets,* was recently published by Amulet Books.

It's about music, love and family. His second novel, *Misfit,* comes out in fall 2011. It's about a demon girl in Catholic school. Visit him at jonskovron.com

**Tara Bray Smith** is the author of *West of Then,* a memoir, and *Betwixt* a novel for young adults. She lives and writes in New York City and Berlin.

Raised in Greenwich Village and Las Vegas, **Daria Snadowsky** is the author of the young adult novel *Anatomy of a Boyfriend.* She has also written for various publications, including *Creative Loafing,* the *Las Vegas Weekly* and the *Nevada Law Journal.* Visit her at daria-snadowsky.com.

**Laurie Faria Stolarz** is the author of several popular young adult novels, including *Bleed, Project 17,* the bestselling *Blue is for Nightmares* series, and the *Touch* series. Her titles have been named on numerous award lists, including the Quick Picks for Reluctant Young Adult Readers list, the Teens' Top Ten pick list, and YALSA's Popular Paperbacks for Young Adults list, all through the American Library Association. Born and raised in Salem, Massachusetts, Stolarz attended Merrimack College and received an MFA in creative writing from Emerson College in Boston. She is currently working on *Deadly Little Voices,* the fourth book in the *Touch* series, published by Hyperion Books for Children/Disney. For more information, visit her website: www.lauriestolarz.com.

**Heather Swain** is the author of the young adult novel *Me, My Elf, & I* and its sequel, *Selfish Elf Wish,* as well as two novels for grown-ups. Her personal essays, short stories and nonfiction articles have appeared in anthologies, literary journals and magazines, such as *Salon, American Baby* and *Other Voices.* When she's not writing, she's often making toys out of stuff around the house, most of which you can find in the book *Make These Toys: 101 Clever Creations Using Everyday Items*. She lives in a crooked house in Brooklyn with her husband and two young children.

**Melissa Walker** is the author of four young adult novels, including the *Violet on the Runway* trilogy and *Lovestruck Summer*. She is cocreator of the popular teen newsletter iheartdaily.com and the awkward-stage blog beforeyouwerehot.com. She still gets crushes regularly, and her husband doesn't mind. Visit her at melissacwalker.com or on twitter.com/melissacwalker.

**Rebecca Walker** is an award-winning speaker, teacher and bestselling author. She presents ideas about race, class, culture, gender and the evolution of the human family that challenge ideological rigidity and encourage fresh approaches to enduring conflicts. *Time* magazine named her one of the fifty most influential leaders of her generation. Her books include *To Be Real: Telling the Truth and Changing the Face of Feminism; Black, White, and Jewish: Autobiography of a Shifting Self* and *Baby Love: Choosing Motherhood After a Lifetime of Ambivalence*.

**Robert Wilder** is the author of two critically acclaimed books of essays: *Tales From The Teachers' Lounge* and *Daddy Needs a Drink,* both of which are in development for television and film. He has published essays in *Newsweek, Details, Salon, Parenting, Creative Nonfiction, Working Mother* and elsewhere. He has been a commentator for NPR's *Morning Edition* and *On Point* and other national and regional radio programs, including the *Daddy Needs a Drink Minute,* which airs weekly on KBAC FM. Wilder's column, also titled "Daddy Needs A Drink," is printed monthly in the *Santa*

*Fe Reporter.* He was awarded the 2009 Innovations in Reading Prize by the National Book Foundation. Wilder lives in Santa Fe, New Mexico, with his wife, Lala, and their two children, Poppy and London. Visit his website at www.robertwilder.com.

**Rebecca Woolf** is the author of *Rockabye: From Wild to Child* (Seal Press, 2008) and the wildly popular blogs Girl's Gone Child and Babble.com's Straight from the Bottle. She is also a panelist on the hit web series Momversation and has been featured in publications, including *Time* magazine, the *New York Times* and *Angeleno* magazine. She lives in Los Angeles with her husband, Hal, and their two children. Visit her at girlsgonechild.net.

# acknowledgments

As always, I have many good people to thank for their help along the way: my lovely editor, Ann Leslie Tuttle; superagent Emmanuelle Morgen; publicity queen extraordinaire Shara Alexander; brilliant web designer Dilyara Breyer; dearest friend Kimberley Askew; and thoughtful editors, Deborah Brody and Gail Chasan.

Thanks to Lauren Cerand, T. Colin Dodd, Amy Dunnigan, Ritu Metzger, Liz Smith, Emily Vassos, Sara Sonnet, Jennifer Mitchell, Sonia Bodilly, Flor Morales, Sangmi Halverson, Caroline Grant, Anne Marie Feld Lowell and the San Rafael Public Library. Much love to my extended family and husband and daughter.

# credits and permissions

## ESSAYS

Credits and Permissions

"Just a Friend" © Brendan Halpin, 2011

"Adam" © Amy Greene, 2011

"My Romantic Past (or What I Heard on My Relationship):
A Mix Tape" © Emily Franklin, 2011

"The Subtle Art of Crush-Suffocating" © Joshua Mohr, 2011

"Olfactory" © Catherine Newman, 2011

"Uncle Greg, a Giant Chicken, and the Murderous Pottery Wheel"
© Heather Swain, 2011

"Giving Up the Ghost" by Melissa Febos originally appeared on
the *Nervous Breakdown* on February 2, 2010

"What Kitty Taught Me" © Christopher Coake, 2011

"Before It Gets Complicated" © Rebecca Woolf, 2011

# about the editor

Andrea N. Richesin is the editor of three anthologies, *Because I Love Her: 34 Women Writers Reflect on the Mother-Daughter Bond; What I Would Tell Her: 28 Devoted Dads on Bringing Up, Holding On To, and Letting Go of Their Daughters;* and *The May Queen: Women on Life, Work, and Pulling It All Together in Your 30s.* Her writing has appeared in *Identity Theory,* the *Huffington Post, Literary Mama* and the *Southeast Review.* Her anthologies have been excerpted and praised in the *New York Times,* the *San Francisco Chronicle,* the *Boston Globe, Redbook, Parenting, Bust, Salon* and *Babble.* She lives in the San Francisco Bay area. Visit her online at www.nickirichesin.com.